LZ-'75

THE LOST CHRONICLES OF
LED ZEPPELIN'S
1975 AMERICAN TOUR

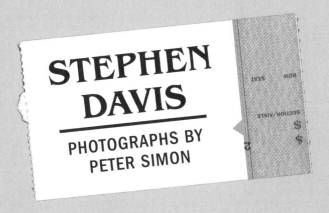

STEPHEN DAVIS

PHOTOGRAPHS BY
PETER SIMON

GOTHAM
BOOKS

GOTHAM BOOKS
Published by Penguin Group (USA) Inc.
375 Hudson Street, New York, New York 10014, U.S.A.
Penguin Group (Canada), 90 Eglinton Avenue East, Suite 700, Toronto, Ontario M4P 2Y3,
Canada (a division of Pearson Penguin Canada Inc.); Penguin Books Ltd, 80 Strand, London
WC2R 0RL, England; Penguin Ireland, 25 St Stephen's Green, Dublin 2, Ireland (a division
of Penguin Books Ltd); Penguin Group (Australia), 250 Camberwell Road, Camberwell,
Victoria 3124, Australia (a division of Pearson Australia Group Pty Ltd); Penguin Books
India Pvt Ltd, 11 Community Centre, Panchsheel Park, New Delhi—110 017, India; Penguin
Group (NZ), 67 Apollo Drive, Rosedale, North Shore 0632, New Zealand (a division of
Pearson New Zealand Ltd); Penguin Books (South Africa) (Pty) Ltd, 24 Sturdee Avenue,
Rosebank, Johannesburg 2196, South Africa

Penguin Books Ltd, Registered Offices: 80 Strand, London WC2R 0RL, England

Published by Gotham Books, a member of Penguin Group (USA) Inc.

First printing, November 2010
10 9 8 7 6 5 4 3 2 1

Gotham Books and the skyscraper logo are trademarks of Penguin Group (USA) Inc.

LIBRARY OF CONGRESS CATALOGING-IN-PUBLICATION DATA
Davis, Stephen, 1947–
    LZ-75 : the lost chronicles of Led Zeppelin's 1975 American tour / Stephen Davis;
photographs by Peter Simon.
        p.   cm.
    ISBN 978-1-592-40589-3 (hardcover)
    1. Led Zeppelin (Musical group)—Travel—United States.   2. Rock musicians—Travel—
United States.   3. Concert tours—United States.   4. United States—Description and
travel.   I. Simon, Peter, 1947–   II. Title.   III. Title: Lost chronicles of Led Zeppelin's
1975 American tour.
    ML421.L4D43   2010
    782.42166092'2—dc22   2010012424

Printed in the United States of America
Set in Warnock Pro
Designed by Sabrina Bowers

While the author has made every effort to provide accurate telephone numbers and Internet
addresses at the time of publication, neither the publisher nor the author assumes any
responsibility for errors, or for changes that occur after publication. Further, the publisher
does not have any control over and does not assume any responsibility for author or third-
party Web sites or their content.

Fan is short for fanatic. *LZ-'75* is hereby dedicated
to all the Led Zeppelin fans, past and present,
memor et fidelis. Non nobis solum nati sumus.

"I ran into pagodas: and was fixed, for centuries, at the
summit, or in secret rooms; I was the idol, I was the
priest; I was worshipped; I was sacrificed. I fled from the
wrath of Brama through all the forests of Asia. I
came suddenly upon Isis and Osiris: I had done a deed,
they said, which the ibis and the crocodile trembled at."
—Thomas De Quincey, *Confessions of an English Opium-Eater*

Prologue

Led Zeppelin rarely let journalists anywhere near the band. Shortly after guitarist Jimmy Page founded the English rock group in 1968, relations with the press deteriorated to the point of outright hostility on both sides. Early reviews of Led Zeppelin's recordings and concerts were negative, unkind, and even vitriolic. Led Zeppelin was described as an unholy amalgam of hype, money, depravity, and Satanism. The band retaliated by banning writers and photographers from their shows, with the exception of a few trusted people who could be counted on to write positive articles and make authorized, band-approved photographs. There were also reliable accounts of journalists being assaulted by members of Led Zeppelin; being spat on; having drinks flung in their faces.

"The press," as it was known, was terrified of Led Zeppelin.

All this changed, somewhat, in 1975. By then, Led Zeppelin was the biggest, highest-grossing rock band in the world, as well as the booming music industry's biggest act. The records shipped platinum. The tours sold out in moments. Zeppelin started a record label, and the products started selling tonnage as well.

But in 1975, the mainstream media didn't play along. The rock press was eager for any piece of Led Zeppelin, but as the band prepared a new album of songs, maybe its best ever, and a sold-out tour of North America, the band's media representatives found certain doors slamming shut and important phone calls unreturned. So it was decided that Led Zeppelin would take the unprecedented step of inviting carefully selected writers, editors, and photographers from the regular media to come along for a taste of the tour from the inside. Backstage passes would be doled out, interviews would be given, a tour photographer was hired. *Rolling Stone* magazine, hated by Led Zeppelin for unfair treatment since 1969, would be courted. An elite from this small constituency would even be offered the occasional seat on "Starship One," Led Zeppelin's flying gin palace, a converted Boeing 727 jetliner, as it ferried the musicians in excelsis, across time zones, state lines, and states of mind.

I was one of those writers.

Between January and March 1975, I covered Led Zeppelin's tenth American tour, as a magazine journalist. I was well treated by the band, its management, and the road crew, and the whole thing was an adventure. Led Zeppelin paid for everything. I heard a lot of great music, and also witnessed concerts that were far less than brilliant, illustrating how a long, hardfought rock campaign could be undermined by illness, exile, homesickness, weather, drugs, and alcohol. In other words, I saw that the current gods of rock were mere mortals after all.

While I was on duty in 1975, I kept three notebooks detailing the daily progress of the Zeppelin tour as I was covering it.

Some entries were more personal, sketching characters I met, and various situations and experiences. On the notebook's covers I scribbled *LZ-'75*. After I wrote my article, I put the LZ-'75 notebooks in a drawer and forgot about them.

Jump ten years to 1985. I'd been searching for the LZ-'75 notebooks for two years because I was writing a biography of Led Zeppelin, which had disbanded five years earlier after drummer John Bonham died. But I'd moved houses, and the notebooks had been misplaced. I had a few details of that period—Zeppelin's most important North American tour—from the manuscript of the old magazine article, but most of the in-the-moment, on-the-road 1975 incidents from my notes were absent from *Hammer of the Gods: The Led Zeppelin Saga*, which nonetheless became an international best seller when it was published in 1985. (I think this happened mostly because, at the time, there was so little available information about Led Zeppelin's twelve-year career. There were no Zeppelin videos on early MTV, and although Robert Plant remained active, he didn't play any of the old songs in concert. In the sudden and complete vanishing of Led Zeppelin after 1980, as if a malign spirit had been banished from the world, millions of rock fans had become obsessed by the legendary band's raw power, addictive charisma, and hellacious mystique.)

Another ten-year jump, to 1995. I was traveling with Aerosmith while collaborating on the band's autobiography. One night in Buenos Aires, Jimmy Page asked Joe Perry to give the induction speech marking Led Zeppelin's entry into the Rock and Roll Hall of Fame that year. Joe enlisted bandmate Steven Tyler to share the speech, and asked me to write it. Joe said he wanted some new material about Led Zeppelin, not a rewrite of *Hammer of the Gods*. Again I searched for the elusive LZ-'75 notebooks, but they were still missing. Somehow, though, I knew they weren't gone, only hiding. I ended up with a speech about Aerosmith's early and slavish appreciation of Zeppelin, voiced by the principals themselves. Steven Tyler, who had begun his career as a drummer, choked up during his tribute to John Bonham. After the evening's speeches, there was one hell of a rock jam in the Waldorf-Astoria ballroom that night.

Ten years after that, in 2005, I finally found the LZ-'75 notebooks. It had been three decades since I had covered Led Zeppelin. The notebooks were in a veritable cardboard 1975 time capsule that also preserved some eight-track tapes, the keys to my old BMW, a ceramic bong, six C-90 tape cassettes of interviews, a thick file of news clippings, Polaroid snapshots and several (now archaic) photographic contact sheets, press releases from the Led Zeppelin office, unused concert tickets, New York subway tokens, a cocktail napkin from the Continental Hyatt House in West Hollywood with scribbled phone numbers, various Zeppelin backstage passes, a letter from William S. Burroughs, a goatskin Moroccan *kif* pouch, and a bundle of teenage fan mail to Led Zeppelin, all dated 1975.

Two years later, Led Zeppelin reunited for a charity concert in London. This single show in December 2007 ignited a planetary wave of interest in the band, with tens of millions reportedly applying online for the 20,000 available tickets. There was a period of intense speculation and hope that this epochal (and famously contentious) group could re-form around the son of its late drummer and reconquer Planet Rock with its dark combo of black magic and Woodstockian fantasy.

But this didn't happen.

Around then, I began to reread the LZ-'75 notes and discovered there was a story that could be told about being around Led Zeppelin at the apex of the band's career. The year 1975 was fateful for Led Zeppelin; an examination of what happened to the four musicians during that year could be intriguing to their legion of fans, a legion that has expanded across three generations. And these were, looking back, extremely interesting times. In America, a president had been forced from office in August 1974 over the pointless Watergate burglary. England was plagued with shortages and strikes, and was routinely predicted to be on the verge of chaos. The Vietnam War was still being fought. It was the era of Idi Amin, Pol Pot, Carlos the Jackal, and ABBA. Jamaican reggae music was fighting an insurgency against disco for the soul of the dance floor. Bob Marley was alive and well. In London, the new punk bands were beginning to rehearse in the back rooms of Kings Road boutiques. But Led Zeppelin, secure within its own secret society, operated outside the temporal runnings; few of 1975's headlines really matter to our story. So I've combined my firsthand account with other reliable sources, some recently discovered, and added musical data informed by the nearly complete library of bootleg recordings of the band's 1975 concerts.

LZ-'75 is a personal portrait of the greatest rock band in history, at the apogee of its flight. For Led Zeppelin, everything they had done until then led up to the epic music they would create in 1975: a year of travel, incredible artistic success, personal exaltation, near-death traumas, and a creative rebirth under painful hardship and dislocation. It was the top year for the band. After 1975, Led Zeppelin would never be the same again.

—S.D.

SWAN SONG.INC.

November 13, 1974

From: Danny Goldberg

LED ZEPPELIN TO TOUR AMERICA BEGINNING IN MID-JANUARY
COAST TO COAST TOUR IS SUPERGROUP'S FIRST IN EIGHTEEN MONTHS

Peter Grant, manager of Led Zeppelin and President of their record label Swan Song, has announced a major American tour for the group beginning in mid-January, and extending -- with a break in the middle -- until the end of March.

This is Led Zeppelin's first tour since their historic 1973 American tour in which they broke several concert attendance records that had been set years before by the Beatles. The most outstanding record set that year still stands: Led Zeppelin attracted the largest paid attendance ever by one act on May 5, 1973 when 56,800 paid to see them at Tampa Stadium in Tampa, Florida. Led Zeppelin consists of Robert Plant, lead singer, Jimmy Page, lead guitar, John Paul Jones, bass and keyboards, and John Bonham, drums.

Shortly before the tour begins, Led Zeppelin will release their sixth album, "Physical Graffiti," on their recently

-more-

444 MADISON AVENUE • NEW YORK, N.Y. 10022 • (212) 752-1330 • CABLE: SONGBIRD

Chapter 1

Cold Night on Boone's Farm

The trouble started, as it often does in Boston, on a freezing winter night. This was in January 1975. The city's radio stations and street papers had announced that tickets for Led Zeppelin's first North American tour in two years would go on sale at the city's main arena, Boston Garden, at ten o'clock on a Tuesday morning.

The kids started lining up on Causeway Street, outside the arena, at six o'clock on Monday night, January 6. They were a young crowd of suburban teenagers—Zeppelin's hard-core audience—and by nine o'clock they numbered around 500. A few had tape players, and songs from *Led Zeppelin, Led Zeppelin II, III,* and *IV,* and *Houses of the Holy* blared in the cold night air.

By ten o'clock, it was ten degrees outside, and someone made the decision to let the kids on line spend the night in Boston

Garden so they wouldn't freeze to death before the box office opened the next morning. A cheer went up as the kids, most of them wearing blue denim, were let into the building.

Soon they were passing joints and swigging from bottles of cheap Ripple and Boone's Farm apple wine. When that ran out, some kids broke into the beer concessions during a shift change of the security guards. Someone opened an exit door and let in a few hundred more kids who had arrived to line up for tickets. The kids turned on the fire hoses and flooded the arena's hockey rink. The police arrived as Led Zeppelin's fans were looting merchandise stands and lighting bonfires composed of the Garden's old wooden seats. Drunken kids then turned the high-pressure fire hoses on the cops and their dogs. It took the riot squad three hours to chase the kids out of the building. The Zeppelin fans then fought the police in the streets until they were dispersed sometime after midnight.

The box office failed to open on Tuesday morning. Damage was estimated at $50,000. A Boston Bruins hockey game was canceled because the rink was fucked up. Then the mayor of Boston, after visiting the sacked and still-smoking arena, declared the city would refuse to grant the local promoter a permit to hold the February 4 concert. Led Zeppelin would be forced to bypass Boston on their 1975 American tour.

When things get out of control, everyone loses money. So promoters in other cities took note. An official from the Ticketron agency, the nation's biggest ticket-seller, contacted Jerry Weintraub, the concert promoter Zeppelin shared with Elvis Presley, and asked him to postpone announcement of ticket sales, but Weintraub refused to go along. In New York, Madison Square Garden managed to avoid a riot by not announcing when Zeppelin tickets would go on sale.

"If we had," a spokesman told *The New York Times*, "the youngsters would have stayed there all week." But demand for Zeppelin's three February shows in New York was so intense that lines began to form in substantial numbers anyway as word leaked out that the box office would open at one A.M. on Sunday morning. Sixty thousand seats for the three shows sold out in three hours. It was reported that 45,000 were sold through the box office and 15,000 sold through Ticketron.

It was different out on Long Island, one of the most passionate of Zeppelin's suburban strongholds. Kids began to line up at the Nassau Coliseum, in Uniondale, three days before the box office opened. To prevent disorder, numbers were assigned to 2,000 people, who were then locked in the hockey arena's exhibition hall and allowed to remain overnight, under guard. In the morning, only the first 900 buyers were able to buy all 20,000 tickets, leading to complaints about scalping and corruption in the ticket industry. When the cops told disappointed fans to go home, there was some shoving and cursing though no arrests.

But two miles away, six fans were arrested when an estimated 2,000 fans jammed into a Macy's department store at the Roosevelt Field mall in Garden City. The line was orderly until twenty-five Nassau County policemen attempted to "reorganize" the waiting line. Some kids at the front of the line were evicted by the cops, and their places immediately filled by others, who seemed to be friendly with the police. Bryan Brett, nineteen, of Glen Cove, told the *Times*: "The cops pushed some of us out of the line, and other kids stepped in front, and they got the tickets while we got nothing after waiting for hours."

Some of the kids told the cops they were crooks and assholes. There was shoving and threats. Six Zeppelin fans were arrested on charges of disorderly conduct and harassment. The

Times reported that "the extent of any ticket scalping for the rock shows could not be determined yesterday. The Department of Consumer Affairs said it had not received any complaints."

Led Zeppelin's entire 1975 North American tour sold out within a few hours after its tickets went on sale. According to Jerry Weintraub, even Evis Presley was impressed.

"Well, I may not be . . . *Led Zeppelin,*" the king of rock & roll would drawl. "But I can still pack 'em in."

Sure, Elvis. Anything you say. Viva Las Vegas.

CHAPTER 2

Key to the Highway

clipped the press accounts of the Led Zeppelin riots from the Boston and New York newspapers because I was currently on a magazine assignment to cover the tour.

This had started the previous month when I received a message that my friend Danny Goldberg had called from New York. Danny was the twenty-four-year-old vice president of Swan Song Records, Led Zeppelin's new record label. I was surprised to hear from him because I'd heard Danny was extremely busy. Swan Song was not only releasing Zeppelin's own albums but was also putting out records by artists that the members of Zeppelin liked. Already signed to Swan Song were Bad Company, a new band made up of young veterans of the English rock scene; Maggie Bell, a bluesy rock belter who was often described as the British Janis Joplin; and the reconstituted Pretty Things, a legendary London band that had started at the same time as the Rolling Stones, playing the same Bo Diddley songs at the same venues as the Stones. Danny's job was to coordinate Swan Song's relations with the press and the media, as well as handle innumerable details concerning Led Zeppelin's upcoming American tour.

I returned Danny's call and left a message with his assistant. I had met him three years earlier, in 1972, when I was an editor at *Rolling Stone* magazine. A mutual friend had told me about Danny wanting to break into the music business in New York and asked if I could assign him a few record reviews so he could build a clip file and tell prospective employers that he wrote for *Rolling Stone*, which at the time was an instant entrée into the booming music industry of the 1970s. I met with Danny at our friend's flat on West 79th Street, and he struck me as a sincere and very spiritual person who knew a hell of a lot about rock & roll and music in general. He was also totally hilarious, had survived a youthful era of contraband and firearms, and had come out of it something of a Hindu/Buddhist angel. I assigned Danny a review of the new comeback album by Lloyd Price, a star of fifties rock & roll, and Danny nailed it. A few clever *Rolling Stone* reviews later, he landed a job with Lee Solters, the doyen of Hollywood press agents, whose main client was, famously, Frank Sinatra.

One day in 1972, Danny flew to Paris with Solters to meet a new client—Led Zeppelin. The band had a serious problem with the rock press, who generally hated them for arrogance, pomposity, "heavy-osity," and especially for their incredible success with young kids. Zeppelin also had a problem with the mass media in general, which totally ignored the band despite repeated attempts to alert the world that Led Zeppelin was outselling the biggest bands of the day—the Stones, The Who, Jethro Tull, and Yes.

Danny explained to Solters that Led Zeppelin had a negative reputation in the rock world. There were widespread rumors in the music industry and its demimonde that guitarist Jimmy Page, whose interest in black magic had been publicized in England, had made a deal with the devil to ensure the band's success. There were stories about some of the band's brutality toward the young women, so-called groupies, who were drawn to them, especially in Los Angeles. Rock writers, notably in England, claimed that members of the band insulted and abused them. A reporter for *Life* magazine claimed she'd been stripped of her clothes and almost raped in the band's dressing room in 1969. *Rolling Stone*'s critics complained that Led Zeppelin recycled old blues songs into bombastic anthems that sold millions without giving credit (and paying royalties) to the still-living bluesmen who wrote the original songs.

In short, Danny explained, Led Zeppelin had the worst reputation of any band in the world. All Danny's friends in the influential New York music media thought Led Zeppelin were wild barbarians, and they were literally afraid of the band.

So, Solters asked, what's our pitch?

Danny told his boss that Zeppelin were extremely famous among their young fans, but now the group needed the mainstream media in order to grow even bigger. He suggested that Led Zeppelin play a few well-publicized benefit concerts during their 1973 American tour, supposedly in aid of a hypothetical blues museum that would supposedly be located in some Southern locale. Solters said he thought this was an okay idea.

Danny and Solters attended Led Zeppelin's sold-out Paris concert at the Palais des Sports that night. As the band blasted into their opening number, "Rock and Roll"—louder than bombs—Lee Solters, a middle-aged man in a suit and tie, stuffed tissue in his ears. Then he leaned over and said to Danny: "I want you to handle this."

The next day, Danny and Solters met with Led Zeppelin's manager, Peter Grant. A huge, flamboyant, ex-professional wrestler, Grant was like the fifth member of the band. He was also feared for outbursts of rage and violence against anyone who threatened his band, to whom he was fiercely loyal. Undaunted, Solters told Grant that he thought they could help with Zeppelin's image problem. Grant glared at him. "What image problem would that be?" Quoting Danny, Solters told Grant that the media thought Led Zeppelin were wild barbarians.

Peter Grant exploded in laughter.

Later that day, Danny and Solters were introduced to Led Zeppelin in a luxurious suite at the Hotel Georges V.

Grant to Solters: "Tell the lads what our image is in America. What was that word you used?"

Solters nodded to Danny, who gulped. Danny to Led Zeppelin: "Well, uh, the press . . . at least in New York, think you're like . . . *mild* barbarians."

The whole band chuckled at this. Brushing long blond ringlets from his eyes, Robert Plant spoke first. He explained that when Led Zeppelin landed in Southern California in 1968, he was nineteen years old, and he just went crazy, but that was all in the past. Now Led Zeppelin were mature family men, successful artists, and all the old tales of groupies and mayhem were gross exaggerations anyway. Now they were looking for someone to tell their side of the story.

Drummer John Bonham was interested in the idea. Hulking, sober, and seemingly benign, he asked the two American publicists if they could help the band reach an even bigger audience—"the people that *don't* know about us?"

Bassist John Paul Jones didn't say a word. To Danny, it seemed as if he didn't even want to be there and couldn't care less what the press, or anyone, thought of Led Zeppelin.

Jimmy Page said very little, other than some bitter remarks about *Rolling Stone* and its persistently negative coverage of Zeppelin, when it covered them at all. Jimmy didn't need to say much, Danny told me later, because "he was just such a star, with the long black hair, the eyelashes, the corrupt choirboy's face. Stardom seemed to radiate out from him."

Danny pitched the blues museum idea, and they seemed to like it. In the end they agreed that Danny would be Led Zeppelin's publicist for their 1973 tour of America. Danny attended every show of the tour, riding with the band on their private jet, Starship One, and helped with the media frenzy when Led Zeppelin's hotel safe deposit box was robbed of $180,000 in New York. When the tour was over, Peter Grant hired Danny to be Led Zeppelin's full-time publicist, working out of the band's Manhattan office on Madison Avenue.

Two years later, Led Zeppelin's 1975 North American tour was looming, and Danny was on the phone to me. "Hey, man, how are you? Do you have a minute? Do you want to come on the road with Led Zeppelin? You do? That's great! Can you get a magazine assignment? You think you can? Terrific. I only need a letter from your editor. Let me know. I'll save you a seat on the Starship. Gotta go. God bless you—good-bye."

CHAPTER 3

Vision of the Future

I had first heard about Led Zeppelin seven years earlier, in the autumn of 1968. I was a university student and the editor of the college newspaper. I knew a guy named Don Law, who had graduated the previous June and was now the manager of the Boston Tea Party, the city's rock venue and electric ballroom. (Don's father, also named Don Law, had produced all the recordings of blues legend Robert Johnson in the 1930s.) One day I heard that a new band from England, the Jeff Beck Group, was playing the Tea Party, so I called Don Law and arranged for press tickets for me and our paper's star photographer, Peter Simon.

When we got to the Tea Party, housed in a former temple in Boston's South End, Don ushered us into the dressing room to meet the band. I was excited because I was a massive fan of the rip-roaring Yardbirds, whose raving, improvised elaborations on the R&B format had revolutionized rock & roll and propelled it into what was being called hard rock. Jeff Beck had replaced original Yardbirds guitarist Eric Clapton a couple years earlier and had now left to go on his own with a new band.

Boston was considered an important tryout town by British musicians because it had a huge student population and the multimedia that catered to it. When Fleetwood Mac arrived from London earlier in the year, they became virtually the Tea Party's house band. Many UK bands started American tours in front of generally friendly Boston audiences who were about the same age as the group. So Peter with his camera and I with my notebook were politely received by brilliant guitarist Jeff Beck, bassist Ronnie Wood, and drummer Mick Waller. Less effusive, in fact completely ignoring us, was the group's young singer, Rod Stewart, who was staring at himself in the full-length mirror, using spit to straighten the ends of his exquisitely shag-cut hair.

The band was nervous. This was a big tour for them, and they were supporting a terrific record, *Truth*, that had several careers depending on its success. We told them we loved the record and played it all the time. The famously moody Jeff Beck loosened up a bit, and Ronnie Wood cracked a few jokes. When the drummer disappeared into the bathroom, Wood informed us that "Wanky" Waller liked to have a quick jerk before playing the show. Rod continued to obsessively tend his coiffure. We were invited to help ourselves to bottles of imported Watneys Red Barrel beer from the ice chest and hang out backstage while the opening band, the Hallucinations, finished their set.

As I was sipping beer, standing against the wall while Jeff Beck and Ron Wood tuned their guitars, my eyes gradually adjusted to the dressing room's low light. After a while, I noticed two figures sitting in a dark corner. One was a huge man of enormous girth, the other a slender figure in velvet clothes and very long dark hair. Don Law explained that the large one was Peter Grant, who managed the Jeff Beck Group. The slender hippie was his other client, Jimmy Page, who had been playing bass with the Yardbirds and was now stepping into the lead guitar role recently vacated by Jeff. Jimmy was joining the Beck tour for a few days to check out the reaction of the American kids to the new, guitar-heavy rock bands emerging from England. Later that winter, Don told me, Jimmy Page was coming back to America with his band, then called the New Yardbirds, playing a new style of heavy rock that people were saying would blow everyone else out of the sky. Peter Grant was just now booking the Tea Party for Page's new band.

That night, the Jeff Beck Group was a smash at the Boston Tea Party. Rod Stewart was so shy in those early days that he usually began the set out of sight, singing his gravel-road lyrics from behind the stacks of Marshall amplifiers. Jeff was incredible, making the guitar howl like a hound and purr like a leopard in heat. In the back of the hall, watching the audience grooving and cheering, stood Jimmy Page and Peter Grant—taking it all in, seeing a vision of the future they would eventually come to own.

Chapter 4

A Giant Hug for Led Zeppelin

Jimmy Page's New Yardbirds mutated into Led Zeppelin during tours of Scandinavia and Britain in the autumn of 1968. The band began its first U.S. tour in late December 1968, playing shows in California and the Pacific Northwest. The band's epochal first album, *Led Zeppelin*, was released early in January 1969.

I had a new girlfriend at the time, and she was a jazz fan. So was her older brother, whom she wanted me to meet. We were on our way to his house when I stopped at a record store in Cambridge and bought Led Zeppelin's album with its iconic cover image of the German airship *Hindenburg*'s catastrophic explosion in New Jersey in 1937.

At the brother's place, while tea was brewing, I asked if I could play my new record, explaining that Led Zeppelin used to be the Yardbirds, one of my fave English groups. They said they didn't mind, so I laid the LP on the turntable, dropped the needle into the groove, and turned the volume up. First came the rumble of John Bonham's leaden wallop, then the unearthly screech of Robert Plant yelling about the days of his youth. This was the first track, "Good Times Bad Times," and it boasted ferocious energy and a Jimmy Page guitar break that made Jimi Hendrix look sick.

I sensed movement behind me. My new girlfriend and her brother were regarding me with horror, their hands covering their ears to escape the piercing wail, the febrile guitar, and the thunderous hard rock. I lifted the needle, replaced Led Zeppelin with *Kind of Blue*, drank my tea, went home, and listened to *Led Zeppelin* under a pair of big headphones.

Immediately, I realized this was new music, an innovative way of making a huge statement with a four-piece rock band. In fact, the term *rock* didn't really apply anymore. Soon, perhaps within a year, a music critic borrowed an idea from writer William S. Burroughs, author of *The Naked Lunch* and other visionary, experimental works, to describe the bone-breaking rhythms, crypto-romantic vocals, and light-and-shade guitar playing that typified this new hybrid of hard rock and the din of battle:

"Heavy Metal."

Led Zeppelin arrived in Boston two weeks later to play four nights at the (completely sold-out) Boston Tea Party. I missed the first night, and heard later their set was plagued by problems with Page's guitar amp. The second night, Friday, began with "Train Kept A-Rollin'" and surged through "Communication Breakdown" and "I Can't Quit You Baby," and on into "You Shook Me" and the stygian depths of "Dazed and Confused," during which Page scraped a violin bow across the strings of his guitar, producing tortured noise from the gaping maw of hell.

They played for two hours, and I left the Tea Party incredibly impressed—and stone deaf.

Led Zeppelin played for three hours Saturday night. By then their street cred was immense, and young rock fans stood outside the Tea Party in freezing weather because the upstairs windows were open so the crowd inside could breathe, and the loud music could be heard two blocks away. Reviews tended to be raves. "After the Yardbirds comes Led Zeppelin," wrote Ben Blummenberg in the weekly *Boston After Dark*. "Rhythms and time patterns shift abruptly. Volume levels change abruptly, yet melodies and chord skeletons merge kaleidoscopically as the band feeds off one another and plays off the ideas thrown out. Intricacy develops out of a form usually quite simple. . . . Led Zeppelin and the Jeff Beck Group are to rock what Formula One cars are to road racing. Their raw power is compelling and hypnotic while their complexity makes repeated exposure a pleasure. Arrangements of the same song vary on successive nights quite widely. As Jimmy Page told me, 'If we can't do it live, we won't do it.'"

I squeezed into the Tea Party for the last Boston show on Sunday night, January 26, which turned out to be one of the longest the band ever played. The old temple was packed to double capacity, with the throbbing light show doing its psychedelic thing and the amplifiers cranked up to eleven. You could hardly move, let alone dance, so it was best to just stand there and absorb the decibel barrage blasting out from the stage.

The notes I managed to scribble read: "Train [Kept A Rollin']" "I Can't Quit You" / "Killing Floor" / "Squeeze My Lemon" / "Dazed" / "Shapes [of Things]" / "Comm. Breakdown" / "White Summer, Black Mountain[side]" / "Babe [I'm Gonna Leave You]" / drum solo (intense!!) / "How Many More Times."

At the end of their regular, hour-long set, the audience went berserk, and Zeppelin came back for an encore. The same thing happened when they tried to leave the stage again, and so they just kept playing—for three more hours. The room was a steam bath. Jimmy and John Bonham had stripped down to hippie-ish crocheted vests. Robert Plant's tie-dyed shirt was drenched. The band's long hair was soaked with sweat. Only John Paul Jones, who didn't move around much, seemed to keep his cool.

Decades later, Jones said the last night at the Tea Party was "the key Led Zeppelin gig—the one that put everything into focus. We played our usual set and the audience wouldn't let us off the stage. We ran out of songs we knew and tried to think of things to play—Beatles songs, anything we might know all or part of. We'd go back on and play anything that came into our heads." (These included "For Your Love," "Long Tall Sally," "Please Please Me," "Something Else," a long Chuck Berry medley, "C'mon Everybody," and dozens of others.)

"There were kids actually bashing their heads against the stage," Jones recalled, "and I'd never seen that at a gig before. When we finally left the stage, we'd played for four and a half hours. Peter [Grant] was absolutely ecstatic. He was crying and hugging us all, this massive grizzly bear hug. I supposed it was then that we realized just what Led Zeppelin was going to become."

Later a disc jockey who was in the dressing room told me that an ecstatic Grant had actually grabbed the four musicians and lifted them all up into the air.

CHAPTER 5

He Cried Twice
That Night

At this point I confess that I missed the last ninety minutes of Led Zeppelin's epic 1969 concert at the Boston Tea Party. Whatever the legend, the band actually sounded ragged (and a little drunk) after three hours, and I wanted to get home to my sexy new girlfriend.

(Years later, I was talking about these Boston Tea Party concerts with Steven Tyler, whose band Aerosmith would follow Led Zeppelin into the breach a few years later. Steven Tallarico, as he then was, had hitchhiked two hundred miles from New York to see Zeppelin's final Boston concert. "I cried twice that night," he told me. "The first time I cried, was because Zeppelin was so fuckin' *heavy* that I had no other emotional way to react to them. The second time I cried, was when Jimmy Page walked out of the dressing room—with the girl I'd been living with in New York, until that moment.")

So I followed Zeppelin's career with mounting fascination

over the next few years as they released records and built an immense audience despite critical disrespect and constant slagging in the rock press.

Led Zeppelin stayed on the road in America for the rest of 1969, recording new music whenever they had a few days off in Los Angeles and New York. So was born that lumbering musical mastodon "Whole Lotta Love" and the other metallic masterpieces on *Led Zeppelin II*, known by some of the band's young fans as "The Brown Bomber" for its jacket art depicting the band as the aircrew of a WWII warplane. Also born in those faraway times was Zeppelin's reputation as hell-raising maniacs. Jimmy Page's interest in (and actual practice of) black magic was the talk of all the famous groupies and their little sisters. The legendary "Shark Episode," in which a willing, naked groupie was poked and prodded with a sand shark that the drummer had caught from the window of a seaside hotel in Seattle, was even set to music by Frank Zappa. By the end of 1969, Zeppelin had set a standard of excess and debauchery that remained unattainable to any band that tried to follow them.

In the following summer, 1970, Jimmy Page and Robert Plant wrote songs in an old farmhouse in Wales, giving the music on *Led Zeppelin III* a pastoral feel of antique landscapes and misty mountains. (The head bangers were still served by rampaging "Immigrant Song" and the sludgy blues of "Since I've Been Loving You.")

In 1971, Led Zeppelin's officially untitled fourth album began its reign as one of the greatest productions of the rock era. "Stairway to Heaven," with its chiming guitars and lighthearted mysticism, became the anthem of its generation and the most requested song in the history of American radio. In 1972, Led

Zeppelin's tours began to outsell even the Rolling Stones, and the band's four albums remained high up in the sales charts. A fifth album, *Houses of the Holy*, came out in 1973 with a garish jacket that spoke of spiritual quests and human sacrifice. Likewise, the band's riotous, high-energy concerts became rites of passage for the youngest members of the postwar generation. Alone among the great rock bands, Led Zeppelin's fans began to identify with the band beyond the music itself. Led Zeppelin, it was generally agreed, had an aura of mystery, mystique, and genius that no other band could touch.

I remained (mostly) oblivious to this. It was totally uncool for a professional rock critic like myself to appreciate Led Zeppelin, whose music was deemed suitable only for cannon-fodder youth intoxicated on cheap wine and pills. As a music editor at *Rolling Stone*, I didn't even know any writer who wanted to touch them. Led Zeppelin was out there, alone, with its crazy young audience: a secret society composed of four musicians, their management and roadies, and about twelve million kids.

That's when Peter Grant hired Danny Goldberg.

So now we're back in January 1975, and I had to get a magazine assignment if I wanted to ride on the Starship. I called a friend at *Rolling Stone* to see how the magazine was going to cover Led Zeppelin this time around. In the past, *Rolling Stone* had mostly ignored Zeppelin's tours, even when the band began setting attendance records for single-act concerts—no one ever opened for Led Zeppelin after they got big—and became known as the highest-grossing band on the planet. But that attitude of the magazine was over when other publications featuring Led Zeppelin on their covers reported sold-out press runs.

Still, *Rolling Stone* would not be punching my ticket to the

Starship in 1975. Already assigned to Led Zeppelin was a teen-age reporter, Cameron Crowe, who had a reputation for writing glowingly positive mash notes about the bands he covered. Clearly, Danny Goldberg had gotten there ahead of me and was taking no chances that a more seasoned rock writer would smear Led Zeppelin once again in *Rolling Stone*.

Who else would give me an assignment? Danny wanted a national publication, so that ruled out my local newspapers. The other national music magazines—*Creem, Crawdaddy, Circus, Hit Parader*—I simply did not want to write for. An editor at *The Village Voice* told me I was out of my mind. So I called my mentor, Bob Palmer, the greatest of the contemporary music writers, who had written for me at *Rolling Stone* and was now the senior pop music critic at *The New York Times*. Bob told me that he had recently written a piece about jazzman Ornette Coleman for *The Atlantic Monthly*, the venerable American po-litical review. There was a young editor there who was trying to inject pop music coverage into the stodgy old magazine. Bob told me that he was treated well, his copy almost untouched, and the pay was good. So I called the editor, Richard Todd, and he invited me to the *Atlantic*'s venerable premises at 8 Arling-ton Street, overlooking the Boston Public Garden. They'd been there for a hundred years.

I was familiar with the *Atlantic* because my father had sold them a couple of short stories back in the fifties, and the maga-zine was a fixture in our household. I was under no illusion that the *Atlantic*—then under the editorship of a former State De-partment hack—was actually going to publish a feature story about Led Zeppelin. But something told me that I really needed to get on the Starship. *The Atlantic Monthly* was still a presti-gious American magazine, and Mr. Todd clearly was on a mis-

DANNY GOLDBERG

sion to try to reach a younger, more with-it audience than the academics and literary types who were the mag's core readership. He had barely heard of Led Zeppelin, so I pitched the idea as the story of a band that was bigger and more important than the Rolling Stones, but no one, outside their high school fan base, knew about it. Richard Todd had heard of the Rolling Stones. He was a nice guy, and I got the assignment.

I called Danny Goldberg and told him. "The *Atlantic*? You're kidding. *The Atlantic Monthly*? What the fuck! Who cares? *You're on the plane.* When can you come to New York? I've just signed a friend of mine to Swan Song; she's really cool, and I want you to hear her."

CHAPTER 6

Hell-Bent for Valhalla

Meanwhile, back in England, rumor had it that no one in Led Zeppelin really wanted to go to America except the road crew. And it wasn't just America. The band was planning to spend the entire year on the road, in tax exile to escape Britain's draconian Inland Revenue. There was talk of playing in Australia, Japan, even South America later in the year.

Zeppelin was six years old now, and the constant touring of 1972–73 had taken its toll. Robert Plant's voice was shot. Sometime after the last show in 1973, he had undergone a secret operation on his vocal chords, which left him unable to speak for three weeks. There were fears at the Swan Song office, on the King's Road in the Chelsea district of London, that Robert's trademark battle cries—hell-bent for Valhalla—and wailing pleas for blow jobs might be more subdued this time out.

Jimmy Page was exhausted from long nights spent mixing the tapes for Zeppelin's new album, which he had finished only the previous November. The tracks dated from as far back as 1971, and equalizing them to sound somewhat alike for an analog record was exacting and time-consuming. Jimmy was also said to be using heroin, which left him weak, anemic, and spectrally thin. And he was anxious about the death threats that Peter Grant told him were being phoned in to the record company and the promoter in America. The threats were, supposedly, aimed not at Led Zeppelin but only at the shadowy guitarist himself.

John Paul Jones had reportedly gone to Peter Grant at the first Zeppelin recording session after the last tour and told him he wanted to leave the band. Jones said he was unhappy with his role in Led Zeppelin and wanted to stay home with his wife and daughters and play the organ in Winchester Cathedral. Grant had told him to go home and think it over. The sessions were canceled, and Bad Company used the studio time to make their first album for Swan Song. Jones arrived at the next Zeppelin session and said nothing about leaving, but to the others he seemed sullen and more withdrawn than usual.

And then there was John Henry Bonham, also known as Bonzo or (behind his back) the Beast. Led Zeppelin's brilliant drummer, the driving pulse of the best rock band on the planet, was miserable about leaving his wife and two children and his cozy farm in the wintry English midlands for three months of touring in America. He was drinking a lot and had put on a ton of weight. He arrived at the only known rehearsal for the American tour; looked fat; drank more than usual; may also have been dabbling in heroin; but played with his usual stomp and drive.

This rehearsal took place at a theater in Ealing, West London, in late November 1974. The atmosphere was light, with a few journalists from the music papers hanging about, and a photographer getting some images of the band sitting on the new drum riser. They first ran through some old rock & roll songs, like Elvis Presley's "Little Sister," and then some of the new songs, especially the one originally titled "Driving to Kashmir." Also tried out onstage were "Trampled Under Foot," "In My Time of Dying," "Sick Again," and "Custard Pie." Then they played "Hound Dog" and "Don't Be Cruel" as a souvenir of their meeting with Elvis after one of his concerts in Los Angeles, earlier in the year.

In the past, Led Zeppelin had never mounted any kind of stage show other than a rock concert by a four-piece guitar band. Jimmy always stood on the right and Robert on the left, with Jones and the drums just behind, the drums on the same level as the group. There had never been a light show, pyro bombs, flashy costumes, or any of the other stagecraft such as working guillotines or the giant inflated penis that Mick Jagger would ride when the Rolling Stones toured America the following summer.

But this Zeppelin tour would be different. Now the drums were up on a riser, slightly above the band. There were costume fittings. Robert would perform in his usual tight jeans with a silken, kimono-like wrap on top. Jimmy ordered expensive, beautifully embroidered stage suits. Burly John Bonham and his drum roadie, Mick Hinton, would dress in identical white boiler suits and black derby hats—the menacing garb of the thuggish droogs in the film *A Clockwork Orange.*

John Paul Jones didn't dress up, but his stage presence was amplified. Once he played only his bass guitar and the Mellotron keyboard, for the spooky bits of "No Quarter." The Mellotron now coexisted with a Steinway grand piano (also for "No Quarter") and a Hohner D6 Clavinet for "Trampled Under Foot."

And there was a new light show, supported by a big truss that had to be built and dismantled for every performance. Laser effects would illuminate the bowed sections of "Dazed and Confused" and the ghostly theremin signals of "Whole Lotta Love." An old-fashioned mirror ball would flicker a million points of light. A huge light sign spelling out L E D Z E P P E L I N was mounted behind the band; it would flash on in a burst of white-hot bulbs only as the band was leaving the stage, reminding the kids that they had just been sandblasted by the world champions of rock.

Everyone agreed that the rehearsal had gone well. Pumping up his team, Peter Grant assured them that the tour would be a blast. It would sell out in ten minutes. They'd all make a fortune. There would be plenty of security, no one would bother them, and they'd all have fun.

Everyone also agreed, privately, somewhat uneasily, that Robert Plant's voice had changed. His range was clearly lower after the surgery on his throat. The operatic Viking wails that began "Immigrant Song" could still be heard up north in Valhalla, but they would never sound as strange and crazy as in days of yore.

CHAPTER 7

A Complex
Die-Cut Affair

aking my assignment seriously, I had to familiarize myself with Led Zeppelin's music. (A friend pointed out that I was a Stones fan, a reggae nut, and a student of Moroccan music. She challenged me on various points of Zeppelin lore—like who gave the band its name. I didn't know. She told me it was Keith Moon.) So I started listening to the Zeppelin albums, in order. First was the Yardbirds' last album from 1967, *Little Games*, on which Jimmy Page had played. Then Jeff Beck's 1968 *Truth*, which featured Jimmy, John Bonham, and John Paul Jones on several tracks. Then Danny Goldberg sent me the entire Zeppelin catalogue on vinyl. I knew—indeed had worn out—*Led Zeppelin*. I couldn't believe what a great rock & roll record *Led Zeppelin II* was—*"with a purple umber-ella and a fifty cent hat."* *Led Zeppelin III* from 1970 was an obvious homage to the important California musicians of the day—David Crosby, Stephen Stills, Neil Young, and especially Joni Mitchell. The untitled 1971 fourth album, the sleeve depicting the old man burdened by the bundle of sticks, had "Stairway to Heaven," which I'd heard too much on the radio but could easily understand why it had become such a teenage anthem. (In America, when a kid died in a car crash, his friends would call the local radio station and ask them to play "Stairway" to coincide with the funeral.) I had never even listened to 1973's *Houses of the Holy*, but I loved the lurid, burnt-orange jacket, the naked children climbing the Giant's Causeway, and the frankly pagan vibe of the music, not to mention such hard-rock masterpieces as "The Ocean" and "Over the Hills and Far Away."

My brother Chris Davis is eight years younger than I. In 1975 he was still in the clutches of ardent Zeppelin fandom. He told me I had to hear the Led Zeppelin bootleg records because the mystical connection between the band and "the kids" was about a communion forged by their intense live shows, which could get very electrical and Dionysian. Chris made sure I got the right bootlegs: *Live on Blueberry Hill* (L.A. Forum 1970); *In the Light* (1969 BBC radio broadcasts); *Unburied Dead Zeppo's Grave* (Japan 1971); *Going to California with Led Zeppelin* (L.A. Forum 1972); and *Bonzo's Birthday Party* (L.A. Forum 1973).

Chris was right. Despite uneven sound quality, the bootlegged concert recordings told more of the story. I could hear the kids yelling stuff at the band, and cheering at the start and end of favorite songs. I could hear Robert Plant talking to the audiences between songs, saying very funny things, and ad-libbing lyrics to the older warhorses. It was now easier for me to appreciate the unusual, semimystical bond between this band and its very large fan base.

Now I began to wonder about the forthcoming, rabidly anticipated new Led Zeppelin album, *Physical Graffiti*. Where was it? It was already mid-January 1975, and the band was about to go on the most lucrative tour of its career. Usually, a rock band would release an album and a 45-rpm single for radio airplay, and then rely on the ensuing tour to draw publicity for the album to pump up sales figures. But Led Zeppelin had a contrarian attitude toward the record industry. Jimmy Page refused to release singles because he didn't like editing and remixing his recordings to sound good on a tinny American car radio. I was fascinated that Led Zeppelin didn't seem to mind going on the road with no new product to sell—on its own new label, no less.

There were good reasons for the album delay. Jimmy had postponed signing off on the final mixes the previous November because they were waiting for some Indian musicians to add some backing tracks to the anthemic new song, "Kashmir." (The musicians never showed up.) The jacket for the double album (two LPs) was a complex, die-cut affair with sliding panels and open windows that took a long time to get right. And with fifteen new songs, Jimmy Page's famous perfectionism guaranteed that *Physical Graffiti* could never have arrived on schedule.

The band shrugged, and went on tour anyway.

On Saturday night, January 11, Led Zeppelin played an unannounced show at the Ahoy, a rock club in the port city of Rotterdam, Holland. This was the first time an audience had heard some of the band's new songs, and if the delivery was sometimes a little ragged, the reception veered between respectful and rapturous. Robert was so nervous after his eighteen-month layoff that he forgot the words to "Stairway to Heaven." Fortunately, the audience knew the lyric and sang it for him.

The consensus in the dressing room was that they had tried to play too many songs the first night.

But it was a shambles the next night in Brussels, Belgium, at the Vorst Nationaal arena. The band was using these shows as open rehearsals, playing without the new light show, again experimenting on the concert versions of "Trampled Under Foot," "Kashmir," and other new songs. They tried out an arrangement of "When the Levee Breaks," which they'd never tried to play in concert before.

But nobody felt well. John Bonham was shaky, very hungover from the night before, and failed to play "Moby Dick," his cannonade of a drum solo. Jimmy Page looked sick, so "Dazed and Confused" was also left out of the set. After less than two hours, Led Zeppelin walked off the stage to sustained applause and demands for an encore, which they didn't play. Jimmy Page murmured to Peter Grant that this band was going to have to pull itself together if they didn't want to get bottled off the stage in America, in just two short weeks.

CHAPTER 8

The True Pride of Led Zeppelin

went to New York in mid-January to set up my coverage of Led Zeppelin. Danny Goldberg wanted me to join the band's entourage for a few days, attend a few concerts, and observe how crazy their fans were for this band. The Swan Song offices were on the top floor of the Newsweek Building, a brick-clad sky-scraper at 444 Madison Avenue in midtown Manhattan. Behind a locked door was a reception area, with a girl answering the phone. The décor was framed platinum albums and piles of cardboard boxes. Danny's big corner office was bare except for his desk, a ten-line phone console, some file cabinets, a sofa, and a large blue statue of Hindu's Lord Krishna playing his flute.

Everyone in the Zeppelin organization had a nickname: Pagey, Percy, Bonzo, Jonesy, Granty. Danny's nickname was Govinda, supplied early on by Robert Plant. "Govinda Goldberg." (This was actually better than Danny's first Plant-bestowed nickname: Goldilocks.)

Danny was taking phone calls, so I gazed out his top-floor window. Looking south, in the wan winter light, I could see all the way to New Jersey. A veteran of the exclusive "back room" at fabled hangout Max's Kansas City on Park Avenue South, Danny was telling a (quite famous) old friend from the Warhol circle that he couldn't have a job with Jimmy Page on the American tour because he was exactly the sort of person that Jimmy hired bodyguards to protect himself from.

Led Zeppelin would shortly arrive in America, and Danny was working twelve-hour days. All the tour media went through him, much of it channeled through the publicity department of Atlantic Records, distributor of Swan Song product. Danny was also one of the links between the band and its booking agents, promoters, and tour operators. Danny was a wonderful young guy with very long hair, a spiritual outlook, and brain-crunching responsibilities. He didn't drink, or smoke pot. He just got the job done. A real New York media pro, he maintained a tight schedule of parties, events, and concerts to attend, after hours. Danny was famous for never staying more than five minutes, but he always showed up.

I'd invited him for lunch, and he was glad to get out of the office for an hour. This was a world before cell phones. On the way to the elevator, we passed a dark office lit only by a yellow lamp. A middle-aged man was talking intently on the telephone. "That's Steve Weiss," Danny whispered. "Our lawyer. Everyone is scared of him."

We ate at an Indian vegetarian restaurant and used the time to block out my dates. Danny suggested I cover Zeppelin's concerts in the New York area at the end of February, and then fly with him to California to cover the Southern California shows, in early March. Danny explained the L.A. concerts were usually the best of the tour, because the musicians were showing off for their girlfriends.

"I thought they were all married," I blurted.

Danny looked at me like I was an idiot.

Could I get an advance copy of the new Led Zeppelin album?

Oy. Danny rolled his eyes. "I have to answer this fuckin' question two hundred times a day. I wish that . . . *I* . . . could get a copy. The release date keeps getting pushed back." *Physical Graffiti* was now scheduled for the third week in February, a month into the tour. The record company guys were upset, nervous, scared for their bonuses. Danny was stressed. Everyone connected to Led Zeppelin was too.

I asked if I could schedule interviews with Led Zeppelin, and Danny just laughed.

"Jimmy? Forget it.

"Robert? Maybe.

"Jones? No way.

"John? You don't wanna know.

"Peter Grant never talks to the press, except a couple guys in London that helped the band in the very early days."

Couldn't Danny have a quiet word with Jimmy for me? It would be hard to get this story published without fresh quotes from the principals of the band.

"It's not impossible," he said, picking up the check. "Think of an angle, and I'll try to pitch it to Jimmy when I see him. And I promise to get the new album to you—as soon as they come in. See you in about a month. God bless."

Back in Boston, I made some calls to friends in London. A few days later, I received, via air mail, two BASF C-90 audio cassettes containing stereo dubs of a vinyl test pressing of what the tape label described as LED ZEPPELIN VI. Included was a handwritten sheet with the tentative song titles and track times. It came from a reporter for *Melody Maker* who shared my fanaticism for Bob Marley and the Wailers, another band at the top of their game in 1975.

That wintry afternoon, I brewed a pot of tea, built a fire, smoked several bowls of crumbly yellow hashish that I had (inadvertently) brought back from Morocco not long before, put on a pair of serious headphones, and plugged the jack into my Sony Walkman Pro cassette recorder. Then I pushed PLAY and cranked the volume.

Side one started with "Custard Pie." In my condition, it felt like I should be behind a blast wall. It had a pile-driving, tone-drop guitar riff, and amounted to another Zeppelin raid on Bukka White's old blues song, "Shake 'Em On Down." Next came "The Rover," slower and very hard, with Robert's plaintive call to his lover "on the far side of the globe," and a massed choir of electric guitars. Robert's plea for generational unity fades away, and then into the slithering, devilish slide guitars of "In My Time of Dying," another appropriation of old U.S. blues. (Bob Dylan had done a version early in his career.) But this "Time" was a twelve-minute sonic splatter painting, so febrile and intense that, after twelve minutes of fiery-furnace musicality, the band loses the moment, and they can be heard laughing at each other.

Whew.

Side two began with the romping "Houses of the Holy," which had been left off the album named for it. ("The Rover" was another outtake from *Houses*.) A noble brute wants to take you to the movies and advises to let the music be your master and to heed the master's call over a loping dance across the landscape.

This was nothing compared to "Trampled Under Foot," a song about a woman and a car that seeks to atomize Robert Johnson's ancient 1936 Ford Terraplane and turn it into a fuel dragster with a 1975 nitrous oxide hookup. I recognized John Paul Jones's clavinet riff right away, appropriated from Stevie Wonder's "Superstition." Led Zeppelin stole only from the best.

"Kashmir" finished the side with eight minutes of orientalism, majestic themes, Himalayan guitar choruses, and an astonishing, authentic sense of wonder. I could sense that the song expressed feelings that simply could not be faked—a real work of art. More than any song, I thought, even more than "Stairway," "Kashmir" sounded like the great masterpiece of the entire rock movement.

Later on, some fans would say that those three songs on side two of *Physical Graffiti* represented Led Zeppelin's finest work. Certainly the three who wrote "Kashmir"—Page, Plant, and Bonham—agreed. Robert later described the epochal song as "the true pride of Led Zeppelin."

CHAPTER 9

Expansive
Spiritual Vistas

took a breather after two sides of *Physical Graffiti*. I made
notes about the intense music I had heard—Led Zeppelin's
latest output, a new chapter of powerful artistry. LZ had to be
the best rock band in the world now. I loved the Wailers, the
Meters, and Little Feat in 1975, but to almost everyone else, Led
Zeppelin was The Shit.

Would it—"rock music"—ever get any better than this?

I put on my sheepskin coat and boots and walked around
the block with the dogs. It was winter in America now, and it
was raining ice. Back inside, I dried the soaking dogs with old
towels. I had another smoke. I made fresh tea, flipped the cassette tape, and waded into side three of *Physical Graffiti*.

"In the Light" was slurry and subterranean, transfused with
sonic weirdness and a harmonium drone created from bowed
guitars. Then it was back to Wales in 1970, with Page's shim-

mering drops of summer guitar on "Bron-Yr-Aur." *Graffiti* then moves forward in time with "Down by the Seaside," from the fourth album's sessions in 1971. "Ten Years Gone" completed the side, a melancholy ballad burst open by Page's rapid fire in the "did you ever really need somebody" section.

On to side four. Led Zeppelin launches "Night Flight" with fiery energy, originally recorded in 1970 and left off what the fans refer to variously as *Zoso, Four Symbols,* and *LZ IV.* "The Wanton Song" was closely related to "Trampled Under Foot" and led into "Boogie with Stu," a rumble through fifties rock with the original sixth Rolling Stone, road manager Ian Stewart, recorded in 1971. Robert Plant sang "Black Country Woman" (from the 1972 *Houses of the Holy* tapes: It was recorded outside in the garden of the old country house they were using as a studio) as if he were complaining about his wife. *Physical Graffiti* ended with a new song, "Sick Again," whose cool, descending guitars seem to emerge from the wreckage of the Brown Bomber, *LZ II.*

Taking the headphones off, I was impressed by how well the band's older material meshed with the newer songs. It told a story about a quest, an adventure that had both transcendent and carnal aspects. The story would be different for everyone who heard it. There would be millions of them, the largest audience in history. Their yearnings would be validated by this music. Their fantasies would be expressed—and respected. The amplified power of the music, its visionary themes, its intense rhythms, and its mystique-laden charm would open expansive spiritual vistas for its audience, far beyond the routines of everyday life. It was a romance, in the best sense of the romantic traditions of the West.

It will, I thought, also be interesting to hear songs like

"Kashmir" and "Trampled Under Foot" performed onstage. I remembered Jimmy Page's words from six years earlier: "If we can't do it live, we won't do it."

Meanwhile, across the Atlantic Ocean, Jimmy Page caught his left hand in the sliding door of a train at Victoria Station and yelped in pain. At first he thought, with not a little relief, that he'd broken his hand, and the American tour would have to be postponed or canceled. But X-rays revealed only a badly sprained ring finger. Peter Grant pointed out that they sold out forty shows in twenty-six cities and would have to give back five million dollars if they canceled. Danny Goldberg issued a press release announcing the accident and that Jimmy was experimenting with a "three-finger fretting technique" so the shows could go on.

Flying commercial from London, Led Zeppelin arrived in Chicago on January 16, 1975, and took over an entire floor of the Ambassador Hotel, overlooking Lake Michigan. Access to the floor was monitored by two former FBI agents. The Windy City welcomed them with the coldest weather ever recorded. Veteran tour manager Richard Cole, one of rock's greatest buccaneers, was dispatched to buy the heaviest fur coats available, but not before Robert Plant's persistent sniffle turned into a cold. Robert's illness was attended by a new member of Zeppelin's entourage, a handsome young doctor who had previously worked for the Rolling Stones and other bands. The doctor carried two large medical cases and was reportedly prepared to treat anything from overdoses to gunshots to homesickness. "Worth his weight in gold," Jimmy Page said later.

The next day, Led Zeppelin flew their chartered jet to Minneapolis, where they spent the evening rehearsing in the cavernous Met Center. They opened the tour the next evening, January 18, with a Saturday night concert that was, Robert Plant apologetically admitted to the kids ($8.50 per ticket), "a bit rusty." The opener, the thunderous "Rock and Roll," was the usual Zeppelin blastoff, but Robert's voice was strained because his cold was getting worse. "Dazed and Confused" was cut from the set because of Page's injury, but Jimmy managed to deliver some sensational blues improvisations that drew loud applause. John Bonham played his drum solo, "Moby Dick," for fifteen minutes. When the band walked off, after two and a quarter hours, and the houselights came on, the kids (who expected a three-hour show) stood and booed for as long as "Moby Dick" had lasted.

Somewhat dispirited, with the tour doctor unnerved because Robert wasn't responding to treatment and felt horrible, Led Zeppelin boarded its Starship and flew back to Chicago in bone-chilling, subzero weather.

CHAPTER 10

Savant of the Occult

Chicago was freezing, well below zero. From the windows of their hotel suite, the band could see that Lake Michigan was frozen over. In a brief phone call, Danny Goldberg told me morale was low in the Zeppelin camp. Robert Plant was now running a fever. The doctor diagnosed influenza and put him on antibiotics. Jimmy Page's hand hurt like hell, and he was drinking Jack Daniel's to deaden the pain. John Bonham was irritated that he had placed below girl drummer Karen Carpenter in *Playboy* magazine's music poll. John Paul Jones was never around, showing up only for the concerts.

The first concert at Chicago Stadium (January 20) was an embarrassment for the band. Robert was trying to perform with the flu, about which he reminded the 20,000 customers five times during the show. (Many girls in the audience realized that they had the same kimono-wrap blouse that Robert was wearing onstage.) "Sick Again" now came right after the opening salvo of "Rock and Roll," and "How Many More Times" was brought from a four-year oblivion to sub for "Dazed." Then the backline—the electric cable that powered the stage—went dead. It took a while to get it right, as Peter Grant fumed with rage at the side of the stage. During a strenuous guitar solo in "Kashmir," a fan up front threw a white sock, which hit Jimmy Page in the face. This was followed by the sock owner's sneaker, but Page was able to duck. The show ended with "Whole Lotta Love," followed by a cannonade of encores: "Black Dog" and "Communication Breakdown."

In the past, the band liked to go back to its hotel for refreshment and then go out to discos and clubs. (Richard Cole later told me he preferred to take the band to gay clubs because no one ever pestered them.) They tried this in Chicago, without Robert, usually the life of the party; the doctor had sent Robert to bed. No one had much fun.

Danny had arranged for Jimmy to speak with reporters from the British press and *Rolling Stone*. These interviews were downbeat, with Jimmy complaining about his injury, the low morale of the tour, and the mediocre concerts so far. He said he was so afraid of flying that he was developing psychosomatic symptoms—vertigo and claustrophobia. It seemed everything was going wrong. "Maybe I'm reaping my karma—at last," he said. Asked if his studies of magic were coming around to haunt him, rock's dark savant of the occult just laughed—darkly.

Both Jimmy and Robert took to Cameron Crowe, who came on like an earnest, worshipful fan. (Later he would be dubbed "Cameron Crowbar" for his ability to pry good quotes out of them.) But he managed to challenge them both. He got Robert to defend his lyrical fantasy world as not being outdated, and still dedicated to peace and love in a world that had become more coarse and dangerous by 1975. Robert, then twenty-seven, spoke about the sadness of growing older and of missing people from the band's early days in Los Angeles, mostly girls who had either died from overdoses or just disappeared.

Jimmy Page told Crowe that he wasn't afraid to die, and that what he was really looking for in life was an angel with a broken wing.

The second Chicago Stadium show (Tuesday, January 21) was better because it had to be. They replaced "In My Time of Dying" (long, unfamiliar) with the delta stomp of "When the Levee Breaks." (Then, according to LZ obsessives, Led Zeppelin never performed this song again.) "Kashmir" was falling into place as the big showcase for Zeppelin's new maturity, and "Stairway to Heaven" drew a massive lighter display—20,000 little flames in the dark—and rolling ovations for its celestial climax. At the opening stutter of "Whole Lotta Love," the audience looked to the musicians like monkeys in the jungle after the bananas had fermented. Jimmy Page started to smile for the first time since he'd left England.

Robert Plant again performed with a fever. After the show he was bundled into a large robe and taken back to bed in his own limo so the others wouldn't catch his flu.

The third Chicago concert (Wednesday, January 22) was the best so far, despite Robert's continuing fever and pain. It was Bonzo, in his white boiler suit, Doc Martens boots, and sinister black derby hat who was holding the band together, providing a steady drive, swinging rhythms, and his basic incredible wallop. Nobody else in music hit the drums that hard. (Robert began introducing him as "Mr. Ultra Violence.") It was a rhythmic foundation that Page and Jones found irresistible to play over. "Moby Dick" may have been a joke or a bore to most people, but

Bonzo would spend minutes playing with his hands, tabla-style, coaxing subtle tonic inflections from the amplified drums. As many wandered off for a piss or a beer, an equal number sat in rapt communion and gave the drummer a raucous standing ovation at the end. Reviewing the show for *Melody Maker* in London, Chris Charlesworth wrote: "It's cold outside, freezing, sub-zero and bitter, but inside Chicago Stadium 20,000 Led Zeppelin fans are roaring in unison as if some giant orgasm has taken over each and every one."

A day of rest helped Robert recover his voice, which still sounded hoarse two nights later in Cleveland (Friday, January 24). But Jimmy's hand hurt less, perhaps because of the quart bottle of Jack he was chugging between songs. The show started cold, with the band playing in a kind of listless fog, but the kids cheered for the pencil-thin laser beams and other light effects. Then, something kicked in, an hour into the set, and the concert took off like a fire truck, sirens wailing. "Trampled Under Foot" was stunning. "Stairway to Heaven" was given a chiming, passionate reading, with Robert's voice occasionally dropping out of tune because he was so ill. But the band was shit-hot for the first time on that tour. A bootleg recording reveals that Robert squeezed a bit of "The Lemon Song" into "Communication Breakdown" at the end of the show. Afterward, riding the Starship back to Chicago, the band agreed that they had played their first semi-acceptable show.

But when Robert opened his mouth to scream the first lines of "Rock and Roll" at the Market Square Arena (Saturday, January 25) in Indianapolis, only a froglike croak emitted from his wild blond head, and the concert, it was agreed by the fans and the local papers, totally sucked.

Peter Grant and Richard Cole huddled with the doctor on

the way back to Chicago. What was the fucking trouble with this guy? The doctor told them that he'd done all he could medically, and the only thing that could help Robert was bed rest and no singing. It was horrible luck. After consulting with Jimmy, Grant canceled the next show, in St. Louis. Led Zeppelin was going to get a few days off so its singer could get his voice back.

CHAPTER 11

Lap of Honor

ater that night, there was a band meeting in Peter Grant's hotel suite. Everyone wanted out of frigid Chicago for three days. Jones suggested the warm Bahamas. Bonham mentioned tropical Jamaica. Jimmy Page wanted to go to Los Angeles to see his girlfriend. Richard Cole reminded the band that the Starship wasn't certified to fly out of the continental United States, so Jimmy got his wish. Everyone packed his bags because the tour wouldn't be returning to its Chicago base—except for Robert Plant, who stayed in the hotel, looked after by the roadies and the tour doctor. Downcast, poor Robert said he felt like he was being punished.

The Starship was a party at thirty thousand feet. They were all thrilled to get out of the deep freeze. The two charming young hostesses kept their drinks topped up, and Jones was urged to play the plane's small electric organ in the bar area. Soon they were all drunk as lords and singing along. Even Peter Grant was bellowing away, to the tune of "Any Old Iron." John Bonham drank an entire bottle of whiskey and was on the verge of blacking out. Richard Cole put Bonham to bed in the jet's rear stateroom, turned out the light, and closed the door.

Chris Charlesworth was on the Starship that night, along with tour photographer Neal Preston. A few years later he told me what had happened next. John Bonham woke up about a half hour out of LAX. The lights had been dimmed, and the passengers were napping or talking quietly. Suddenly, the bedroom door opened and John Bonham staggered out, wearing nothing but a robe. Still roaring drunk, he lurched forward and grabbed one of the girls and started groping her, mumbling something about sexual intercourse. She tried to break loose, but he put her in an arm lock. She screamed.

Suddenly, Grant and Cole were on Bonzo like two linebackers. (The enormous Grant had been a professional wrestler.) They dragged him off the girl and back into the bedroom and slammed the door. Chris didn't know what was happening in there, but suddenly, Grant came out and took the crying girl in his arms. She was known to idolize Jimmy, so he was deputized to talk with her and get her calmed down so there wouldn't be any problems later on. The rest of the flight passed without incident. Just before the Starship landed, Richard Cole had a quiet word with Chris and Neal, indicating his extreme (and dangerous) displeasure if anything about this unfortunate episode leaked to the press.

Richard Cole later told me that there were two John Bonhams. One was "Bonzo," a great pal and full of fun. The other was "The Beast" (behind his back), as in "There's a party later? Don't tell The Beast." The Beast was a psychotic bully who attacked people and then was ashamed when he found out about it later. It was a real problem when Led Zeppelin went on tour. No one could predict when The Beast would surface, but it usually happened when John Bonham was drinking and desperately homesick for his family.

They went straight from the airport to Zeppelin's home away from home, the Rainbow Bar & Grill on the Sunset Strip, where they were seated in the cordoned-off VIP area. After a few minutes, a drunken musician came up and began shouting at Jimmy Page. *"You can't fucking play guitar! Fuck you!"* This went on for a while. Normally, Richard Cole would have throttled this person—he once kicked someone's teeth out in similar circumstances—but Cole had gone on to the hotel with the luggage. So a weary Peter Grant got up and hauled the drunk out to the alley by his collar. Grant kicked the man and was about to land a crippling punch when he was approached by a young girl with a pen in her hand, who sweetly asked, "Excuse me, Mr. Grant? Can I please have your autograph?"

The tour checked into the Continental Hyatt House on Sunset Boulevard, known locally as the Riot House when Led Zeppelin was in town. Jimmy huddled with his girlfriend as the two FBI guys kept watch outside the door of his suite.

A few days later, on Wednesday, January 29, the band was woken at an obscenely early hour to make the cross-country flight to that night's gig in Greensboro, North Carolina. Five black Cadillac limousines rented from a funeral home drove them to the sold-out Greensboro Coliseum with a police escort. Hundreds of ticketless fans were milling around the backstage entrance. Richard Cole predicted they would be a security nightmare later on, when the band had to make their getaway.

There they learned that Robert was still very hoarse, although feeling better. To lessen the strain on his voice, they cut "The Wanton Song" from the set and then played a show that the audience seemed to find boring. Halfway through, Richard was told that a riot was going on outside. Hundreds of kids had tried to storm the building, fought the cops with bottles and rocks, and were now destroying the three limos that had been left outside. It was a scary scene, and the two limo drivers in the backstage area tried to resign, along with their cars. Grant offered to buy them, right then, for cash. They said the cars didn't belong to them. So the road crew was gathered, looking like a biker gang with knives on their belts, and Grant threatened to flip the limos on their backs if he couldn't have them.

Greensboro was a real runner. Less than a minute after finishing "Communication Breakdown," Richard Cole stuffed the band and himself into the first limo. Grant shouted, "I'm driving," and dragged the driver from his seat. The rest of the tour—nine people—crammed into the second car with roadie Magnet at the wheel. The police escort in front of them was slow to move, so Grant started bumping the big Cadillac into the back of the squad car until the escort got the message. The police cars cleared a brief path through the riot in progress as the cars were pelted with debris and bottles. Then they were on the highway, police sirens wailing, with Grant speeding through red lights and swerving through heavy traffic, everyone laughing like mad or screaming in terror. When they got to the private aviation section of the airport and saw their plane all lit up and fueled and ready for them, Grant did an extra lap of honor around the big jet. "Fucking useless piece of junk," he shouted at the car as he kicked in the door panel. "My old Bentley goes twice as fast!"

Led Zeppelin was airborne five minutes later, being served cocktails and canapés. Early the next morning, they checked into the Plaza Hotel in Manhattan. The hotel's management had demanded a $10,000 security deposit before the band's reservations could be confirmed.

CHAPTER 12

Journey to Middle Earth

Led Zeppelin had Thursday off. Jimmy's suite was kept darkened, curtains drawn, lit only by candles. He complained that the faux Louis XVI décor was tacky. John Paul Jones's suite had been supplied with a grand piano. A high-ranking diplomat from the Soviet Union, who was staying at the hotel, indignantly demanded to be moved after John Bonham blasted deafening records in the suite above him, keeping the ambassador awake all night. Robert Plant took his evening meals at Nirvana, a nearby Indian restaurant that overlooked wintry Central Park. He kept reminding the waiters that his wife was of Indian descent.

Danny Goldberg had a meeting with Jimmy to pitch a magazine story. *Crawdaddy*, the rock mag published in New York, was offering to put Jimmy on its cover if he did an interview with writer William Burroughs, with whom the magazine was starting to work. The sixty-one-year-old writer had recently returned to America from a long European exile and was living in a downtown loft. Danny explained that Burroughs was keen on the idea, but he didn't want to do a Q&A interview with Jimmy Page. Rather, the writer proposed, they would meet, have a drink, go out to eat, and tape the conversation, from which Burroughs would compose an essay.

Jimmy accepted immediately. William S. Burroughs was, with Jack Kerouac and Allen Ginsberg, one of the legendary Beat writers. Like Jimmy Page, Burroughs was fascinated by magic, black or white, in all its forms. Like Page's hero Aleister Crowley, Burroughs was a savant himself, interested in human sexuality, weird science, and methods of social control. It was agreed that Bill Burroughs would attend one of the New York concerts, and then he and Page would meet for dinner sometime after that.

The next night (Friday, January 31), the Starship flew to Detroit, where Led Zeppelin had sold out Olympia Stadium. "Good evening," Robert Plant greeted the audience after the first three songs. "It's great to be . . . *just about* . . . back." Sounding hoarse, he explained the band's health issues: his flu, Bonzo's tummy ache, Jimmy's finger. The set had started very strong but sputtered out after "Kashmir." Bonham wasn't feeling well and wasn't playing his best. "How Many More Times" didn't crunch like it should, and Robert had lost most of his upper vocal range. People noticed that he was singing two octaves below the 1973 levels, and that indeed his febrile voice had changed.

The flight back to New York was subdued. Jimmy was locked in the aft bedroom with Peter Grant. John Bonham was slumped in the lounge up front, probably drunk. Near him was a promo man from Atlantic Records, Danny Marcus, who had made the trip to Detroit with the band. Marcus may have been talking too loud or said the wrong thing, because, with no warning, The Beast reached over and grabbed Marcus's eyeglasses off his totally shocked face. The Beast broke the glasses in half and ground them into the orange shag carpet with his boot. Then, without a word, John Bonham got up and walked to the back of the plane.

Richard Cole had seen the incident, and tried to explain to the shaken promo guy that this kind of thing happened when Bonzo had been drinking and was missing his wife and kids, and not to take it personally. Danny Goldberg later asked Bonham if he might apologize, reminding him how important the promotional people would be for the success of *Physical Graffiti* when the new album finally got into the record shops. Bonzo said he would, but then he didn't.

Led Zeppelin was better the following night (Saturday, February 1) at Pittsburgh Civic Arena. By now the lighting crew had refined their effects, and the audience seemed entranced when a thick fog of dry ice spread over the stage as Jones played the doomy Mellotron theme to "No Quarter." When the lurid little neon-colored laser beams cut through the fog, there was loud cheering. As the last notes of "Communication Breakdown" closed the concert, the giant L E D Z E P P E L I N sign flashed on behind the drum riser. One lighting technician's job was to change the sign's five hundred bulbs after every show.

It was a bright winter late morning in New York City. Danny Goldberg sat in his office high above Madison Avenue, stuffing complimentary press tickets into envelopes for the upcoming Zeppelin concerts in Manhattan and on Long Island. I was helping him, and pestering him to get me an interview with Jimmy

Page. Danny insisted this could not happen. He promised me Robert Plant when the tour got to Los Angeles, but there was no chance Jimmy was going to talk to *The Atlantic Monthly*, an American publication of which he had never heard. Jimmy, Danny told me, was holed up in the Plaza Hotel with Bebe Buell, a beautiful girl who had been a *Playboy* Playmate the year before. (She usually lived with rocker Todd Rundgren. The photocopied daily tour bulletins referred to her as "Mrs. Rundgren.") Since the dripping wax of ten scented candles had destroyed his hotel television, Jimmy had rented a projector and was screening a silent 16mm version of Kenneth Anger's underground movie *Lucifer Rising* because he was supposed to be working on the music for its sound track.

The seats Danny gave me for Led Zeppelin's first Madison Square Garden concert (February 3) were in the loge, to the left of the stage. This was my first Zeppelin show since the Boston Tea Party six years before. Also in attendance, like me on a magazine assignment, was Bill Burroughs. "My first impression of the audience," he noted, "as we streamed through one security line after another—a river of youth looking curiously like a single organism: one well-behaved clean-looking middle-class kid." Burroughs and his entourage were seated in the thirteenth row, near the stage. The big room went dark, and then exploded as Led Zeppelin lit into "Rock and Roll." The crowd sat down to listen to the new song "Sick Again," but then jumped up and danced to epochal "Over the Hills and Far Away," a riff-banging journey to Middle Earth. "Good evening," Robert said after this, his voice a hacksaw rasp. "Whatever happened to nice warm weather? Well . . . maybe we can overcome it tonight, eh?"

"In My Time of Dying" was a real stoner trance, but it was new to the young audience. I noticed a lot of kids going to the bathroom. "The Song Remains the Same" got them back into the room. "The Rain Song" drew massive cheering. (These were the big songs from Zeppelin's 1973 tour.) The new centerpiece, "Kashmir," was also unfamiliar but was received with the respect it obviously deserved. The dry ice fog and laser lights deployed during "No Quarter" drew a good response.

"Trampled Under Foot" got the fans out of their seats, followed by the long stretch of "Moby Dick"—almost sixteen minutes that night. "How Many More Times" was dropped, having bombed in Pittsburgh. "Dazed and Confused" was back in the show, along with the violin bow and the pencil-thin lasers. "Stairway" was given its due, with its fan-based display of lighters swaying in the dark. Then "Whole Lotta Love" tore it down, followed by a (rare for this tour) jam on the encores. "Black Dog" was interrupted by a bit of "The Crunge"—Led Zeppelin's homage to James Brown—and an old Yardbirds riff. "The Lemon Song" was again snuck into "Communication Breakdown." The kids roared at the familiar sounds. The first New York show was a big success, but a half hour of Led Zeppelin had been cut from the halcyon days of 1973. The Zeppelin fans took notice of this in their 'zines.

Richard Cole ordered a runner. But some fans and photographers had set alight some trash cans and tried to block the backstage exit so the limos could be slowed down and photos could be taken, but the experienced New York drivers crashed right through the flaming barrels and raced north to the Plaza Hotel.

CHAPTER 13

Hot Tea with Lemon, Please

here were two parties after Led Zeppelin's first Madison Square Garden concert. I got into the first one, held at the Penn Plaza Club adjacent to Madison Square Garden. This was a crowded melee thrown by Atlantic Records chairman Ahmet Ertegun, the reigning don of the record industry, and attended by various Rolling Stones, Keith Moon, William Burroughs and friends, plus Andy Warhol with an entourage of edgy downtown denizens. Jimmy Page arrived (two hours late) with "Mrs. Rundgren" on his arm, a girl so beautiful that the men forgot to breathe for a moment when she walked into the room. I had hoped to meet the band, but the musicians were sequestered in a private area guarded by Richard Cole, and only Andy Warhol (wearing his platinum wig) and some glam-looking girls were getting through. I left after an hour. Danny told me later that Ronnie Wood approached Jimmy, who had recently absconded with Wood's wife, and blithely asked him, "How's our bird?"

Later, I heard there was an after-party that went *very* late. Ron Wood invited some of the band ("Don't tell The Beast") to the deluxe apartment of Freddie Sessler, a friend of Keith Richards, whose claim to fame was a close connection to a Swiss pharmaceutical company, and a valid license to import weapons-grade cocaine into the United States. This very private affair was held behind closed doors, with a restless Mick Jagger maneuvering through the darkened hallways. Extra girls—some of them reportedly still in diapers—idled in the main salon. One very young chick, obviously starved for attention, played with a buzzing vibrator.

People magazine was, in 1975, America's chief arbiter of celebrity. The day after Zeppelin's first New York concert, the new issue featured the band on its cover, over the headline: LED ZEPPELIN–THEY'RE BIGGER THAN THE BEATLES!

On Tuesday evening, February 4, I drove out to Uniondale, on Long Island, to see Led Zeppelin play at the Nassau Coliseum. It was seriously cold, and steady snow was falling on the hot muscle cars—Camaros, Mustangs, GTOs—"Detroit Iron"—in the vast parking lots around the arena. My tickets were down front, so I got a load, so to speak, of Robert Plant's tight jeans and floppy kimono top, which revealed an obvious tumescence and a lot of bare male breast. A burly line of security guards made sure no one got into the pit beneath the lip of the stage, although several kids tried, in vain. Robert's voice wasn't in great shape, and his preening and prancing seemed exaggerated when seen up close, as if to compensate for some strange frequencies he managed to produce on the high notes he was obliged to sing. As in days of yore, Robert inserted a few lines of the old hippie anthem "San Francisco" into "Dazed and Confused." I timed the concert at 2:25.

After this show, it was snowing so hard on the Grand Central Parkway that it took me an hour to drive the twenty miles back to my digs on Park Avenue.

Two nights later (Thursday, February 6), I wanted to get on the Starship for the Montreal show, but Danny was taking some Japanese rock press to see the band, and the plane was full. The Starship landed in an arctic whiteout. From the limos, they could see that it had recently snowed about ten feet. Robert lost most of his voice between the airport and the Montreal Forum.

"Can someone make me a hot tea with lemon?" Robert croaked as he walked into the dressing room. Jimmy Page's hand still ached, and he was swigging from a bottle of Jack. Jones huddled with the techs because the Mellotron—a crucial element of "No Quarter" and "The Rain Song"—was playing too slow. Tour photographer Neal Preston was shooting this backstage scene and would work that night's show as well.

Led Zeppelin again failed to ignite on that freezing night in Canada. Third song in, Jimmy's guitar amp went out. Long delay. After a wobbly "Rain Song," Robert tried to explain that the Mellotron's prerecorded tapes (that simulated a cheesy string section) were really too fragile to be hauled around North America. "In fact," he went on, "we're going to try to simulate some Eastern violins just about . . . now." This led into "Kashmir," which was emerging as the artistic centerpiece of the concerts, even though the song was completely unknown to the kids. But the "Kashmir" renditions were getting better every night as the tour progressed, as Led Zeppelin became accustomed to playing, and displaying, its monumental new anthem for its core audience.

Robert introduced John Bonham as "Karen Carpenter." Huge cheer.

Playing his famous red Gibson double-neck guitar, Jimmy's solo on "Stairway to Heaven" was (maybe) the best on the 1975 tour, according to Led Zexxperts who have studied all the available bootleg recordings made that year.

"Black Dog" had always been the first encore. Tonight "Heartbreaker" replaced "Communication Breakdown" as the second. It was a hot performance. The kids were bonkers, jumping up and down. "Good night, Montreal—you're the best," Robert called as he left the stage. Then he turned back and said, "You guys are so hot, maybe you've melted all the snow around the hall."

Back in New York, Led Zeppelin had been invited to a party for the Jackson Five, but they got back past the superstar Motown group's bedtime. David Bowie was waiting for them at the Plaza, though. Jimmy said a quick hello and then went up to Bebe Buell. Robert and John Paul Jones spent some time with the former Ziggy Stardust, currently appearing in his persona of the Thin White Duke, possibly testing Peruvian alkaloids, before retiring themselves.

Mick Jagger was hanging around the tour now, because the Rolling Stones were going on the road in the 1975 American summer, playing the same venues as Zeppelin, and Jagger wanted to study Peter Grant's managerial methods. Robert Plant was very proud of a pink message slip saying that "Mr. Jagger" had telephoned him at the Plaza. Mr. Jagger was very present, and quietly observing, backstage, at the second Madison Square Garden show on Friday, February 7. Robert's vocals started hoarsely but got better as the show proceeded through a flow that was by then becoming semi-normal to the band. Bonzo's "Moby Dick" solo was edging up to the twenty-minute mark, and the kids down front (no large video screens in those days) sensed that the burly drummer would happily play all night, if asked to. Robert introduced "In My Time of Dying" by telling the audience that, considering the band's ill health, it was an apt title. Again the final encore was "Heartbreaker."

CHAPTER 14

Aware of the Energies

A few nights later, in a Mexican restaurant in the East Village, William Burroughs was talking with Jimmy Page about one of the old writer's favorite subjects: crowd control. How do you maintain a sustainable balance in the concentration of mass human energy that you get at a rock concert? Jimmy Page allowed that, indeed, sometimes things could get pretty tricky.

"One has to be aware of the energies that you are going for, and . . . you could so easily . . . I mean, for instance, the other night [Saturday, February 8], we played in the Spectrum in Philadelphia, which really is . . . a *black hole* of a concert hall. The security there is the most . . . ugly of anywhere in the States. I saw this incident happen and I was almost physically sick. In fact, if I hadn't been playing the guitar I was playing, it would have been over somebody's head. [This was during 'Stairway to Heaven.'] It was a double-neck, which is irreplaceable, really, . . .

unless you wait another nine months for them to make another one at Gibson's."

Burroughs asked Page to describe the incident.

"What had happened, somebody [left his seat and] came to the front of the stage to take a picture or something, and—obviously—somebody said, 'Be off with you.' And he wouldn't go. And then one chap [security goon] went over the barrier, and then another, and then another, and then another and they all piled on top of . . . you could see the fists coming out, on this one solitary person. And they dragged him by his hair and were kicking him. It was just sickening."

At that point, an angered Robert Plant stopped singing about a bustle in your hedgerow and began shouting at the goons to stop beating the crap out of this poor stoned kid. The kids up front were screaming at the goons. Jimmy stopped the show and walked around, his guitar hanging, visibly upset. Robert went to the lip of the stage and bopped one of the goons on the head with the base of his microphone stand. These burly shirts turned around and started glaring at Robert, who was trying to re-store the stuporlike calm that had prevailed in Philadelphia until then. "Can we advocate that people stay in their seats?" he pleaded. "It's not very pleasant to see situations like this, right under your nose . . . so . . . can we all keep cool?"

Led Zeppelin restarted "Stairway to Heaven." Soon, in the wings, Richard Cole nudged Peter Grant. There, on the other side of the stage, was the security guy Robert had bashed, and he was cursing and rubbing his bleeding head. Grant finished his third bottle of Blue Nun wine. Richard Cole and some of the road crew grabbed the man and rushed him out of the building, where they had a frank discussion with him in the alley. The encore was short, and the band was out of the hall and into the cars before the amps stopped buzzing.

The point Jimmy later tried to make to William Burroughs was about maintaining a balance of control. "Now, what I'm saying is this: Our crowds, the people that come to see us, are very orderly. It's not the sort of . . . Alice Cooper style, where you actually *try* to get them into a state where they've got to go like that. [In Philadelphia] the wrong word said at the wrong time, could've just *sparked off* the whole thing."

Led Zeppelin never performed in Philadelphia again.

Led Zeppelin flew their jet to Baltimore two nights later (Monday, February 10) and played a workmanlike concert at the Capital Centre in nearby Landover, Maryland. As Jimmy Page's hand began to heal, "Dazed and Confused" was getting better every night, with lots of improvised harmonics and tone-drop rhythms. The kids cheered every time the lights went on and a spotlight revealed Jimmy bowing his electric guitar, eliciting stygian growls and demonic shrieks, as if to draw the Dark One from his lair in hell. Invariably, some of the more astute of Led Zeppelin's listeners realized that what they were watching was in part a magic show.

Others were fighting each other and the cops, both inside and outside the hall. The Baltimore press reported more than twenty arrests for assault and vandalism, and twenty others were taken to the hospital. It was said to have been the most unruly and violent crowd the police had ever seen at a local rock concert.

Led Zeppelin's third 1975 Madison Square Garden concert (Wednesday, February 12) took place after twelve hours of heavy, wet snow had blanketed Manhattan. The band's limo convoy swerved and sloshed from the Plaza to the venue in a foot of slush amid a serious blizzard. "Good evening," Robert greeted the sold-out hall after the third song, explaining they had to drive forty blocks in a storm to get there. "Today, people were calling up and asking, 'Is it gonna be on?' For a minute, I was wondering about my anatomy. . . . Then I realized, there was some . . . discrepancy about the weather." Robert went on to say that he appreciated how the deep snow slowed down the vibe of the great city, and how cool that was.

He had also taken to addressing the fans about still-unreleased *Physical Graffiti,* before introducing the set's fourth song, "In My Time of Dying." This was unfamiliar to the kids, and the band was frustrated because the audience seemed distracted while they were playing an important new work they were proud of. So Robert explained that tonight, they were playing songs from their entire career, and please give the new stuff a good listen. As for the new album? "As usual, it's late. But we don't want to do too much [of the new songs] . . . in case you all get fed up with it."

The concert was one of the best of the 1975 tour. The unfamiliar "Kashmir" almost played the stars out of the sky, and received a huge ovation from an audience hearing it for the first time. The band got loose in the encores, slipping a funky version of Elvis Presley's "That's All Right, Mama" into the "Heartbreaker" encore.

"Thank you! Thank you! . . . Ladies and gentlemen of . . . *New York*! [Massive extended cheering as Led Zeppelin, arms clasped around each other, took their final bow] You're . . . *too much*! [Sound of firecrackers and cherry bombs going off.] And if I may say so . . . ha-ha . . . *We ain't so bad ourselves!*"

BONHAM

CHAPTER 15

The Magus of
Franklin Street

ed Zeppelin had a few days off while they were in New York, so they put on the heavy coats bought for them in Chicago a month earlier and ventured forth into the snow and slush of winter. Robert shopped at record stores in Greenwich Village. Jimmy Page hung out with guitarist Joe Walsh (who presented Page with a very rare Les Paul model guitar). Together they attended a Linda Ronstadt concert at the Capitol Theater in Passaic, New Jersey. John Bonham drank like a fish and had a stomachache. The tour doc suggested to John that he modify his alcohol intake, and just got laughed at. No one ever knew where John Paul Jones was.

Tour photographer Neal Preston had the assignment to photograph the band for the cover of *Rolling Stone*, something that Jimmy Page was determined to subvert because he hated the paper's previous (mostly contemptuous) treatment of his band. Neal set up a room at the Plaza for the shoot, and Robert,

Jones, and Bonham showed up at roughly the appointed hour, but not Jimmy Page. Danny Goldberg ran up to Page's suite, but Bebe Buell said he had gone out.

After an hour of frantic searching—the paper's staff in San Francisco were holding the cover, waiting for the photograph— Page finally showed up with his arms full of dead roses. He told Danny that he'd been looking for black roses but couldn't find any. The dead roses expressed his scorn for *Rolling Stone* and especially the critics who'd slagged Led Zeppelin. Preston shot a roll of color film and sent it off to California by overnight air freight. But when they tried to develop the pictures, all they could see were some dark images that looked like ghosts, as if Page's negative energy had contaminated the film stock. (Eventually, *Rolling Stone* used one of Preston's concert shots on its cover, which appeared later in the month.)

The long black limousine carrying Jimmy Page to his encounter with William Burroughs made its way down Fifth Avenue in a light snowfall. The car stopped in front of 77 Franklin Street in a dark, shabby neighborhood of vacant or abandoned industrial lofts that were slowly being reclaimed by young artists and urban pioneers. Jimmy was greeted at street level by James Grauerholz, Burroughs's young assistant, who led Page up four steep flights of stairs to Burroughs's loft. The sixty-one-year-old writer, dressed in a coat and tie set off by an embroidered Moroccan vest, extended his hand and offered his guest a cup of tea, which Page happily accepted. Also on hand was a photographer to document the interview, and *Crawdaddy*'s publisher, Josh Feigenbaum, whose idea this meeting had been. Before getting down to business, Burroughs proudly showed Page his orgone accumulator, which looked like a big plywood crate. Sitting in this box, Burroughs explained, concentrated certain energies in a productive and healthful manner according to theories developed by the psychiatrist Wilhelm Reich. Jimmy Page declined Burroughs's offer to give the orgone box a try.

Burroughs thought he and Jimmy might know people in common since Burroughs had lived in London for most of the past ten years. It turned out to be an interesting list, including film director Donald Camell, who worked on the great *Performance*; John Michell, an expert on occult matters, especially Stonehenge and UFOs; Mick Jagger and other British rock stars; and Kenneth Anger, auteur of *Lucifer Rising*. Burroughs told Page about the feelings of energy and exhilaration he experienced sitting in the thirteenth row of a Led Zeppelin concert. These feelings, he told Page, were similar to those he had known while listening to music in Morocco, especially the loud pipes and drums of the Master Musicians of Jajouka. Page somewhat sheepishly admitted that he had yet to visit Morocco but had been to India and Thailand and heard a lot of music there.

Burroughs was interested in getting Page to speak about crowd control, a longtime fascination. "It seems to be that rock stars are juggling fissionable material of the mass unconscious that could blow up at any time," he pondered.

"*You* know, Jimmy," he continued. "The crowd surges forward . . . a heavy piece of equipment falls on the crowd . . . security goes mad, and then . . . a sound like *goddamned* falling mountains or something."

Page didn't bat an eye. "Yes, I've thought about that. We all have. The important thing is to maintain a balance. The kids come to get as far out with the music as possible. It's our job to see that they have a good time and no trouble."

Burroughs launched into a series of morbid anecdotes he'd collected about fatal crowd stampedes, like the 360 soccer fans crushed to death during a riot in Lima, Peru. Then there was the rock band Storm playing a dance hall in Switzerland. Their pyro effects exploded, but the fire exits had been chained shut. "Thirty-seven people dead, including all the performers," Burroughs recalled.

He poured two fingers of whiskey for himself and for Page. Burroughs had been informed that these were the first Zeppelin shows to deploy any special effects. "Sure," Page said. "That's true. Lights, lasers, dry ice are fine. But I think, again, that you have to have some balance. The show must carry itself and not rely too heavily on special effects, however spectacular. What I really want is laser . . . *notes.* That's more what I'm after. Just . . . cut right through!"

Burroughs then wondered if the power of mass concentration experienced by Zeppelin's audience could be transposed into a kind of magic energy that could materialize an actual stairway to heaven. He added that the moment when the stairway becomes something physically possible for the audience could be the moment of greatest danger. Page again answered that a performer's skill involved avoiding these dangers. "You have to be careful [with large audiences]," he said. "It's rather like driving a load of nitroglycerine." Page described the fan abuse they had seen in Philadelphia a few days earlier as an example of a situation that could really crack, but somehow didn't.

Over margaritas at the nearby Mexican Gardens restaurant, Burroughs asked about Page's house on the shores of Loch Ness in Scotland, which had once belonged to Aleister Crowley. Was it really haunted? Page said he was sure it was. Does the Loch Ness monster exist? Page said he thought it did. Skeptical, Burroughs wondered how the monster could get enough to eat. The conversation continued over enchiladas. Burroughs talked about infrasound, pitched below the level of human hearing, which had supposedly been developed as a weapon by the French military. Then on to interspecies communication, talking to dolphins via sonar waves. Burroughs said he thought a remarkable synthesis could be achieved if rock music returned to its ancient roots in ceremony and folklore, and brought in some of the trance music one heard in Morocco.

Jimmy Page was receptive. "Well, music which involves [repeating] riffs, anyway, *will* have a trancelike effect, and it's really like a mantra. And, you know, we've been attacked for that."

They parted company on the icy sidewalk outside the restaurant, with many thanks and good-byes. Jimmy Page's limo, which had been waiting for him, whisked him back to the Plaza Hotel. William Burroughs, James Grauerholz, and Josh Feigenbaum walked back to Burroughs's loft to listen to the tape that Josh had recorded of the conversation.

Chapter 16

Drones and Cones of White Noise

rctic weather conditions prevailed, but the fans streaming into the arena were buoyant with excitement. A full-throated human crowd roar greeted the band as I watched Led Zeppelin take the stage of the Nassau County Veterans Memorial Coliseum on Long Island at eight o'clock on Thursday, February 13. "Rock and Roll" opened the show and scalped the first twenty rows of raving suburban kids. Jimmy Page was in an expansive, jazzy mood, cutting sly riffs out of familiar concert patterns. "Dazed and Confused" got the violin bow treatment, producing scary, droning cones of white noise. My favorite moment of any Zeppelin show was when, in the middle of "Whole Lotta Love," a roadie rolled out Jimmy Page's antique theremin, an early electronic "instrument" that was basically a radio receiver. Page's shaman-style hand gestures, toward and away from the theremin's antenna, elicited insane shrieks and interplanetary sonic whorls that sounded incredible over the thunderous bottom of Jones and Bonham. It was an astonishing spectacle, probably unique in the history of rock concerts. I thought it was one of the coolest things ever.

For several shows, Jimmy had been performing in one of his new stage suits. This was a black silk two-piece wizard's garb, with appliquéd moons, stars, suns, and ringed planets. The trousers sported long silver cuffs worn over white-topped black loafers. Another new costume, known as the dragon suit, was said to be waiting for him in Los Angeles. However, for the New York shows, Page mostly dressed casually in light-colored bell-bottom trousers and a black-and-silver shirt. His mane of hair was getting really long, and it flew about as Page performed his hieratic, gunfighter's dance with his guitar.

Led Zeppelin had, from its earliest days, a firm policy of no opening acts and no jamming with outside musicians during shows. But the crowd seemed thrilled as Ron Wood, who would replace Mick Taylor as lead guitarist when the Rolling Stones toured later in the year, strolled out for the second encore. While the roadies were plugging in Rockin' Ronnie, Robert sang snatches of "Roll Over Beethoven" and Elvis Presley's "Teddy Bear." Then "Communication Breakdown" was revived and extended so both Page and Wood could solo. Wood was properly deferential: He was no Mick Taylor, and anyway, no guitarist in his right mind would attempt to outdazzle "Magic Fingers" Page on his own stage.

The next day, with one New York area show remaining, there was some minor dissension in the ranks. The band had been away from home for more than a month, and some of them were getting cranky. The whole year abroad in tax exile looked much better on paper than it felt in (what passed for) reality among the members of Led Zeppelin. John Bonham and John

Paul Jones were now complaining that the spotlight never stayed on them except during their extended instrumental solos. Jones also complained to Danny Goldberg that he was never included in interviews, and asked why this was so. Danny tried to placate Jones but couldn't bring himself to tell the moody bass player that no one wanted to interview him. About the spotlight issue, Danny tried to have a quiet word with Jimmy Page, who told him to speak to Showco's lighting director, who in turn advised Danny that he was under strict orders from Jimmy that neither Jones nor Bonham should be lit up while the whole band was on the stage.

John Bonham was getting extremely homesick. He and his roadie/slave Mick Hinton (who carried a supply of diapers with him because Bonham became incontinent when he drank to excess) were usually to be found well oiled. The band was also having trouble with the hotel phones, making it difficult to call their wives back in England. This enraged John Bonham, who liked to speak to his wife, Pat, every day if he could, and he would fly off the handle, break things, or take it out on the faithful Hinton.

Led Zeppelin was back on Long Island the following evening (Friday, February 14). It was so cold my usually trusty BMW 2002 wouldn't start. I had to ride the Long Island Rail Road to nearby Hempstead and take a taxi to the Nassau Coliseum. As usual after the first three songs, Robert walked to the front of the stage. "Good evening," he said, his voice almost normal. "Today is almost the last of the old pagan rites to survive into the twentieth century. Now they call it St. Valentine's Day. . . . Yeah, it's a day for sowing our wild seeds—ha-ha." He went on to explain that they would be playing new stuff, old stuff, all the flavors of "the glorious ice cream cake of Led Zeppelin."

Robert went on to mention that Led Zeppelin had enjoyed its visit to New York and would now be moving on. "Despite our depleted physical conditions," he added, "we fully intend to shake this building." The crowd so far had been fairly quiet. "And you know, *we can't shake this building by ourselves!*"

But the kids seemed sedated by the long, dense atmospherics of the unfamiliar "In My Time of Dying." And Jimmy continued the downer mood when he called for the metallic blues, "Since I've Been Loving You," which Led Zeppelin hadn't played on this tour. A bit later, an unusually soporific Zeppelin performance was made even less intense by the long, long cocktail jazz stylings of J. P. Jones during his big nightly showcase, "No Quarter." It was as if Jones were determined to have his (long) moment in the spotlight because it was the only moment he ever got.

The mighty Led Zeppelin, the highest-grossing band in the world, never caught fire that night, and neither did the Nassau Coliseum. Crunching "Heartbreaker" was back as the last encore, but the bored customers were already leaving the building and heading for the ice-covered parking lots. Several reviewers described the concert as "the St. Valentine's Day massacre." There were zero cabs to be had, so I walked the two miles to Hempstead in freezing rain, and caught the last train back to Penn Station.

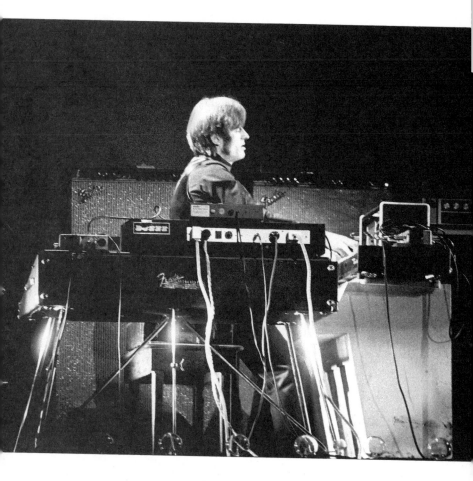

JONES

Chapter 17

A Spiritual Quest

Led Zeppelin had a day or two off. Danny Goldberg said he'd heard that some of them went to the movies. The young bartender of the Plaza Hotel's famous Oak Bar told me he'd heard that Jimmy Page had been awake for three days. Films within walking distance of the Plaza Hotel included James Caan in *The Gambler*, Peter Falk in *A Woman Under the Influence*, and Charles Bronson in *Death Wish*. (Years in the future, Jimmy Page would write the sound track to *Death Wish II*.) Showing on Eighth Avenue was the double bill *Deep Throat* and *The Devil in Miss Jones*. On Friday, February 16, 1975, the band packed their luggage and flew the Starship to St. Louis, where they played a concert at The Arena, a big old barn of a hall, a concert that had been canceled in January when the doctor said Robert Plant was too sick to perform.

From the opening notes, Led Zeppelin grabbed St. Louis by the throat and kept its grip for the whole night. Even the new songs from the still unreleased *Physical Graffiti* drew standing ovations from a sold-out audience that never sat down for almost three hours. Shit-hot "Trampled Under Foot" had everyone jumping up and down. The intense stomp and floral bouquets of "Kashmir" drew rapt attention, as if these fans understood that this new anthem with an Eastern accent could challenge mighty "Stairway to Heaven." "Dazed and Confused" featured bowed improvisations during which Page cranked up a few bars of "Train Kept A-Rollin'," an ancient text of the Zeppelin canon.

The band encored with simian "Black Dog" and saurian "Heartbreaker" and then did a runner for the limos. The Starship was airborne by midnight, bound for New York, where Led Zeppelin split up during a ten-day break. John Paul Jones and John Bonham flew home to their families in England. Robert Plant and Jimmy Page retreated to a private house on the Caribbean island of Dominica, a tropical paradise where it would be impossible, according to all accounts, for Page to score any heroin.

While the gods went on vacation, I went home to type my notes on the Led Zeppelin tour thus far. A few days later, my editor at *The Atlantic Monthly* rang up to ask how the assignment was going. He also said that the magazine would want to see photographs of the tour. I told him I'd take care of it.

But it was going to be a little tricky.

Photographer Peter Simon, with whom I'd gone to see Jeff Beck at the Boston Tea Party in 1968, was still my colleague and friend. We did magazine jobs and newspaper features together. He shot the pix with his Nikons and Canons and I typed the words on my Smith-Corona electric portable. We made a meager living at it, and had some fun too. So it was natural that I'd call him about Led Zeppelin. But something held me back.

The previous summer, there had been an uncomfortable rift over a girl. Peter and I had both been living in dilapidated old fishing camps on Martha's Vineyard. I was writing record reviews and newspaper columns, and he was taking pictures of girls on the famous nude beaches in the remote, western end of the island. We played tennis every day, tried to stay high, and in general were living as best we could. Then one day in July, Peter told me that our old friend Peggy Day was coming to the island for a visit. This was exciting because Peggy was extremely hot: slim, petite, lithe, an ecstatic hippie child dancer. She had been Peter's girlfriend back in college when she was a precocious seventeen-year-old out of Stuyvesant High in New York. They had stayed together as a couple and moved to a hippie commune in Vermont. During this period, Peggy and I had a secret tryst at the farm that, because it was so transgressive, was the most torrid one-night stand of my life.

Peter and Peggy broke up somewhere around 1972, and she disappeared, having lit out for the territory. A postcard to me had been mailed from Santa Cruz, California. We'd last heard that she was in Central America, where she'd gone on a spiritual quest of some kind. So it was good to know she was alive and coming to visit Peter. He was living alone; maybe their old love would rekindle. It was a beautiful concept. But then she moved in with me instead.

I'd gone to Boston for the day, and when I returned to the island on the midnight freight boat, Peggy Day was lying there—in my bed, really beautiful in the glow of a glass oil lamp. Beautiful, but also damaged. She was rail-thin and dark brown, her blond hair very long and braided for bed. We talked a little.

She said she was hitchhiking up-island on her way to Peter's but decided my house was closer, and she knew the key was in the mailbox. She said she'd been through hard times in Guatemala. She said she was now twenty-four years old. She said she needed looking after. I had a girlfriend who was off in graduate school for the summer, so I told Peggy to get some rest, and I had a cold shower and slept on the daybed in the parlor.

The next day, she went to see Peter, and I figured I'd see Peggy at the beach. But they didn't show up. That night was a hot one, and I went to bed early with *Tender Is the Night*. An hour later, I heard soft footsteps, the screen door opening, and there she was, slipping out of her summer dress, turning down the wick of the oil lamp until it was too dark to read. We made love in the morning as well.

So Peggy Day spent about three weeks in my care, which is the only way I can put it. She had come to the island to recover from some trauma she had suffered. She was very quiet, preferring not to be specific about her experiences in Guatemala. She needed to eat fresh food, swim in the warm sea, walk in the cool woods every day, and be looked after. She was indeed quite spooked and stayed close by my side every day she was with me. Later, she told me that she'd gone to Central America with a boyfriend, but he had somehow died. I couldn't get much info from her. She was more a mysterious presence than a person.

After a week, Peggy had gained some weight and developed a healthy glow. After two, she'd become voluptuous again, and was turning heads when we went into town. She liked being driven around the island in my old blue BMW, her long hair streaming in the breeze. At home she moved around like a sylph, soundlessly, making clever arrangements with the wildflowers she picked. I bought her some watercolors at Alley's Store, and she began painting again. When she smiled, it was like diamonds and sunrays. But she had her darker moods, too, and when she was in one of them, it was a good time to make love to her. She said that it helped.

Through all this, I managed to stay friends with Peter. He had several other girlfriends anyway, and it was all over between him and Margaret Day. Then summer began to wane, and my girlfriend was coming to the island. Peggy said she wanted to stay and live with us, maybe have a child. I told her that my girl-friend might kill both of us. There were tears, and not hers alone, as I drove her to the ferry.

After that, I didn't see Peter for a while. Then, around the time I needed a photographer, I got a postcard from him in Los Angeles, which is exactly where I would be covering the Led Zeppelin tour in a fortnight.

So we worked it out. Peter Simon and I were on the job once again. The story was Led Zeppelin, and we had to get the goods.

CHAPTER 18

In Our Glory

Led Zeppelin regrouped on February 26 in Houston, Texas, where the band and its management had supper together at the Whitehall Hotel. The next evening, they played a brilliant show at the Sam Houston Coliseum. "Rock and Roll" had dragster drive supplied by a recharged John Bonham. The local reviewers wrote that the kids just went crazy. "Sick Again" was an explosion of metallic crunch. "Over the Hills and Far Away" shuddered the building. After the third song, Robert greeted the audience: "Good evening, Houston. Welcome to an evening of . . . madness. We've been off for a few days . . . but now we're back, and *we are in our glory!*"

But Robert's voice still sounded raw and throaty. He was still singing an octave lower, which deprived some of the songs of the manic flash of the recorded versions. But the singer's sense of humor remained in top form as he introduced John Bonham as "our protean percussionist—the Lord of the Droogs—a man you never want to meet in a dark alley." Plant also changed his homage-to-hippie interlude during "Dazed and Confused," jettisoning the hoary "San Francisco" fragment and substituting a verse and chorus from Joni Mitchell's "Woodstock" anthem instead.

Jimmy Page also had some new tricks for the tour's second leg. The theremin came out during the *sturm und drang* of "Whole Lotta Love," and—provoked by Page's artful hand gestures—emitted its unpredictable palette of wicked, eerie radio waves. As Bonham powered through the song's driving polyrhythms, Page again dived into the rarely performed "The Crunge"—Led Zeppelin's homage to James Brown and his great guitarist, Jimmy Nolen. The encore was "Black Dog," and long after the band had left the hall, its fans were still on their feet, waving their lighters and cheering.

Physical Graffiti had finally been released by Swan Song Records on February 24, while Led Zeppelin was enjoying their mid-tour hiatus. The double album's jacket art depicted New York tenement buildings (96 and 98 St. Mark's Place) with die-cut windows that revealed alternative scenes (including Robert Plant and Richard Cole in drag costumes) when the record sleeves were interchanged. With the unstoppable momentum of a rolling brownstone, Led Zeppelin's new music was an instant sensation. In America, *Physical Graffiti* debuted at number one on *Billboard* magazine's crucial sales chart, and remained at the top position for ten weeks. (*Physical Graffiti* is said to have been among the first record albums to gain "platinum" status—a million units sold—on advance orders alone.) In America, the album also debuted at number one on both the *Cash Box* and *Record World* charts. Likewise, Canada's *RPM* chart. Likewise, *Melody Maker*'s chart, and all the others in England. Also Japan,

Germany, France, Italy, Scandinavia. Then all five previous Led Zepp albums started to sell, earning respectable chart positions, years after their initial release. Then Swan Song's other albums— especially Bad Company's hard rocking record—began to chart as well. By the time Zeppelin went back on the road at the end of February 1975, they were not only the biggest band in the world, but their fledgling record company was the hottest label on the planet as well.

Robert Plant started talking about *Physical Graffiti* in his remarks to the audience at the band's concert at Louisiana State University in Baton Rouge on Friday, February 28. Before playing "In My Time of Dying," Robert explained that the unfamiliar song was on Led Zepp's new album, which had appeared in the record shops after weeks of frustrating delays. "The egg has . . . *finally* been laid," he exclaimed. Bonzo yelled some remark that made Plant laugh. Then he added: "Or was I . . . the guy that got laid? Oh, well—no matter." Later, he introduced Bonham as "the guy with the bicycle clip stuck in his sock—the greatest percussionist since Big Ben." He also teased John Paul Jones about his new look, as Jones had returned from vacation with his familiar long mop of hair trimmed to a much shorter length. (Jimmy said that he thought Jones looked like Liberace, the camp piano showman who was a big draw on television and in Las Vegas.) At the end of the show, after "Black Dog" had its say about the supposed lack of soul among big-legged women, Robert thanked Baton Rouge for being a really good audience. (After threats were reported against the supposedly Satan-friendly band, extra security had been laid on by the promoter. The papers reported next day that three pistols and more than twenty knives had been confiscated at the gates.) Led Zeppelin was, he told them, "just a bunch of fun-loving guys." With that, the Starship flew to New

Orleans, where the tour checked into the Le Pavillon Hotel, and Led Zeppelin had the weekend off.

Then it was back to Texas, where the audiences had always been rabid for the band. They played the Tarrant County Convention Center in Fort Worth on Monday, March 3. A somewhat revived Jimmy Page plunged into "Whole Lotta Love" for all he was worth and played its changes for thirty-five minutes, expanding the theremin section with tortuous war whoops and rhythmic static. "The Crunge" was fast and furious, and the band received a standing ovation even before the encore.

This ecstatic reception was missing the following night when Led Zeppelin began a two-night stand at Dallas's Memorial Auditorium (Tuesday, March 4, and Wednesday, March 5). The first night, the three-song barrage got only tepid applause. Plant was shocked. "Dallas? Come in? Are you receiving us? If you ain't, . . . we'll make sure that you will. . . . And we've got two nights to do it." His voice was hoarse, though, at times little more than a croak on the higher notes. "I'd like to bid you all good health," he told the kids, who were still sitting on their hands. "I'd like to bid *myself* good health as well." There was some pallid applause. Then, dripping with sarcasm, he cautioned the zombie-like Dallas crowd not to go crazy. "Don't get too . . . *atmospheric* on us, okay?"

During the central section of these shows, John Paul Jones would move to the Mellotron for "The Rain Song," and then stay on the cheesy synthesizer for majestic "Kashmir." Then, introducing the band, Robert advised that "John Paul Jones played the Mellotron, a rather cheap form of orchestration—and he doesn't cost much to rent, either." Robert wasn't through. "John

Paul . . . since he'd had his hair cut, has taken to watching the Liberace show on television . . . He [Jones] also plays the organ at Blackpool [a seaside resort comparable to Atlantic City] during the summer season in England."

Led Zeppelin responded to the narcoleptic Dallas audience by playing what the band considered a mediocre show. Usually, even the most docile audience cheered for John Bonhams's twenty-minute "Moby Dick" solo, but not in Dallas that night. Robert kept trying to get the crowd going. After "Trampled Under Foot" failed to blast off, he pleaded, "Come *on*! Why don't you all . . . wake up?" After even "Stairway" failed to register, Robert chided the customers. "It feels terrible to look out at an audience where everyone is . . . so flat faced. These days, there doesn't seem to be much smiling going on."

After this show, most of the tour checked into a hotel in Dallas, but Jimmy, Robert, and Peter Grant flew the Starship back to New Orleans for the night. The mood on the big jet was flat for the hour-long flight. It had been a long night, and it hadn't gone very well.

CHAPTER 19

Little Red Corvette

The next day, John Henry Bonham woke up in his hotel suite in Dallas sometime after noon. He was probably hungover, and his digestive problems made him grumpy. So the god of rock stars smiled on Bonzo and provided an instant morale booster. The first thing the drummer spied when he looked out the hotel window was a customized 1959 Chevrolet Corvette, gleaming cherry red and creamy under the gray, overcast Texas sky. It was parked beneath his window in the hotel's driveway. Bonzo was a car nut, a hot rod fanatic. He was drooling over the sexy Texas 'Vette.

Later in the day, Bonham was being driven around Dallas by one of Zeppelin's new security team, a moonlighting FBI agent from Boston named Jack Kelly. When they returned to the hotel, the Corvette was still parked near the lobby. As he was going up to his room, Bonham said to Kelly: "Jack—I want you to wait by this car until the owner comes for it, and then I want you to tell him that Mr. Bonham would like to buy him a drink. And—if he won't come—see if you can have him arrested."

Kelly relayed this to Richard Cole, who found the Corvette's owner through the hotel and put him together with Led Zeppelin's voracious drummer, who could easily afford any vehicle he fancied. Bonham was clearly besotted by this car, a notoriously loud and uncomfortable land rocket that could do about 180 mph on a flat track. By the end of the afternoon, Bonzo had agreed to pay about $18,000 in cash, that day, for a car that was worth no more than $10,000.

The simple concept of John Bonham driving his new toy in America was an immediate problem for the Zeppelin entourage. His driving license had been suspended in England for more than a year, due to numerous (and egregious) speeding offenses. The previous owner had taken the car's plates with him, so the Corvette was now unregistered and uninsured—a disaster waiting to happen. Bonham wanted only to take his new baby out for a spin, almost begged for it, but Richard Cole—backed by Peter Grant—wouldn't let it happen. Led Zeppelin's lawyer, Steve Weiss, was forced to spend an (expensive) afternoon at the Dallas automobile registry, trying to get the car certified, but some of the paperwork was dodgy, and it didn't happen. Bonzo was able only to drive the Corvette into the hotel's garage, and then periodically visit the machine to rev its powerful engine for the benefit of select members of the road crew. Later that week, Richard Cole arranged to have Bonzo's vintage Corvette trucked to Los Angeles, where the car was stashed in the garage underneath the Continental Hyatt House on Sunset Boulevard until its proud new owner arrived a few days later.

• • •

The second Dallas concert was better. The audience was dancing in the aisles this time, and Led Zeppelin turned the heat on. After "Over the Hills and Far Away," Robert told them that it was great to be back in Texas "even if me and Pagey been flying back to New Orleans every night." This drew a few catcalls, so Robert tried, "Tonight? I don't know. . . . Whatever happened to the Butter Queen?" (This referred to a notorious Texas groupie that Zeppelin had encountered back in the early days. She was part of a talented sisterhood of rock star devotees that had included the Plaster Casters from Chicago and Dahlia the Dog Act in Los Angeles.)

Before introducing "In My Time of Dying," Robert explained that it was from their new album, which just happened to be at the top of the charts—"and we're grateful and happy about it." He arduously promoted *Physical Graffiti* throughout the show, sniffed some of the lacy underwear that girls were tossing onstage, scolded an overzealous security guy who was rough with the kids who only wanted to take an up-close snap with their Instamatics. He introduced the drummer as "someone who can go for hours without stopping. But . . . [muffled] . . . he's still a lousy lay." After the show, the Starship returned to sultry, more fun New Orleans once again.

Now Led Zeppelin's tour experienced a gap, because a massive outdoor concert scheduled for the West Palm Beach Raceway in Florida on Saturday night (March 8) had been canceled the previous week when the promoters failed to meet the band's financial terms on time. Danny Goldberg issued a press release pointing out that Led Zeppelin was extremely disappointed because in 1973 the band had played its biggest show to date in Tampa, Florida, where they set a record for the largest concert ever played by a single act. The mayor of Miami then offered the Orange Bowl as an alternative site—if the concert could in part benefit a local charity for sick children. Attorney Steve Weiss wrote to the mayor, expressing the band's appreciation of this gesture but explaining that the short time span prevented Led Zeppelin from mounting "a proper and artistic concert" for March 8.

Peter Grant filled this gap by accepting a last-minute booking in Austin, Texas, for Friday, March 7. The show in the sophisticated Texas university town had sold out within minutes, so Led Zeppelin flew in and played a fast and furious concert. The new "Kashmir" drew thunderous applause, the best response the unfamiliar song had drawn on the tour thus far. This would increase now, for the rest of the tour, as fans had the opportunity to hear the recorded versions of "Kashmir" and "Trampled Under Foot" (the first single and radio grenade from the album) before hearing them in concert.

Robert's voice was in much better form in Austin, and he continued to shamelessly plug *Physical Graffiti* and tease John Paul Jones for his haircut. John Bonham was introduced as "your worst nightmare from *A Clockwork Orange.*" For the encore, roadies set up another drum kit, which was then manned by hard-hitting Simon Kirke from Bad Company. This double-drum barrage launched "Whole Lotta Love" into orbit and then "Black Dog" landed hard on the lighter-blazing crowd of kids.

The band did a runner to the airport after the show and piled into the Starship. Spirits were high because Led Zeppelin was finally heading west to its spiritual home and subtropical playground of Los Angeles for the crucial Southern California leg of their 1975 American tour. Three of the four members of the band had girlfriends waiting for them. And it was well known that Led Zeppelin always played at the top of their form in L.A.

CHAPTER 20

The Smiling Dog Saloon

A week prior to this, I was flying aboard an Eastern Airlines 727 jet, on the way to Cleveland with Danny Goldberg to cover a club concert by the first American artist signed to Swan Song Records. She was a New Age spiritual singer who styled herself "Mirabai," after a sixteenth-century Indian saint.

Her real name was Karla Major, and Danny had discovered her singing original songs at a large weekly group meditation in a church basement in downtown Manhattan. Danny's own spiritual awakening had taken place around the time I met him in 1972, when he came under the influence of the American guru Ram Dass (formerly Professor Richard Alpert of the Harvard psychology department). Ram Dass had directed Danny toward the meditations organized by Hilda Charlton, a middle-aged devotee of Hindu dance. Danny became engrossed by the fierce devotion, the healing prayers, and the spiritual music offered at her sessions at St. Luke's parish church, amid the sail lofts and warehouses of

Hudson Street. I'd been to a few of these meditations, which drew a diverse crowd of seventies New Yorkers: hippies and beatniks, corporate business types, disco-looking kids, street people, bearded academics, and housewives from Queens. Prayers were offered chiefly to Lord Krishna and other Hindu divinities, but Hilda was catholic in her beliefs, and when necessary she could also throw in St. Francis, Chief Joseph, Lord Buddha, and any other saintly ray of light that might help someone's intractable cancer or whatever. Danny told me a secret fantasy was to get Robert Plant to one of Hilda's sessions, as he thought it would be a natural fit for the singer, who was interested in spiritual quests.

Music, singing, clapping, and declaiming were an important part of Hilda's meetings. When I attended, it was hard not to be swept into the fervor of her flock. It was there that Danny first heard the devotional songs of Mirabai, an attractive young woman of about twenty-five who was writing songs proclaiming her love for blue Lord Krishna. Danny heard something profound in the songs of this latter-day Mirabai. He offered to manage her career, and since Swan Song Records was coming into being late in 1974, Danny arranged with a temporarily pliable Peter Grant to have her debut album recorded and released on Led Zeppelin's new private label—an enormous coup for an unknown singer.

Now Mirabai was out on the road, playing rock clubs in secondary music markets, trying to get a buzz going before recording her album in Nashville. Danny had invited me along to Cleveland, where his client was playing that night at the Smiling Dog Saloon, a rowdy blues bar in the suburbs. After our flight landed, we took a taxi to a Holiday Inn near the club. Danny huddled with Mirabai for a while, then invited me to his room to meet her. She was pretty, petite, and attractive, with dark hair and a wan smile. She was exhausted from trying to get her earnest songs over to beery bar patrons who really just wanted to party down. Danny told her he knew this was a slog for her, but it was part of paying dues that every professional musician had to undergo at the beginning of a career.

The Smiling Dog Saloon was packed on Saturday night, March 1. Many patrons were inebriated, and the room was teeming with sweaty bodies, noise, and cigarette smoke. I mentioned to Danny that this venue seemed an odd fit for Mirabai, and he explained that a successful gig at a place like this was good exposure and could influence radio airplay when her album came out. Indeed, Danny had gotten Cleveland's rock stations to hype Mirabai's gig, using the Zeppelin connection as a lure, and the city's radio and media elite duly turned out for her show.

Mirabai took the stage at nine o'clock with her guitar, and—after a respectful hearing of the first two songs, both odes to determination and spiritual enlightenment—she was then completely ignored by the crowd for the rest of the evening. Mirabai never had a prayer, but she gamely carried on, trying to get the chattering, laughing drinkers on her side.

Finally, Mirabai stopped singing because she couldn't hear herself over the saloon's din. People in back were shouting for boogie music. At a front table, a young man who'd been listening ardently, giving her some hope that she was at least reaching someone, suddenly collapsed into his beer and fell off his chair, coming to an inert rest under the table. But Mirabai was nothing if not a trouper. "You know," she told the audience, "when Lord Krishna played his flute, dozens of pretty milkmaids would come around and want to have fun with him. To keep them all satisfied, Krishna had to split himself into dozens of Krishnas, so there'd be enough to go around. Now, if any of *you boys* can pull off *that* trick, see me backstage after the show."

The following week, while Led Zeppelin played their Texas shows, I hung around the Swan Song office in New York. Danny and I would fly to Los Angeles later, in time to cover the Southern California shows. With Steve Weiss traveling with the Zeppelin, and with Danny dealing with the fallout from the canceled Florida concert, the atmosphere in the band's office was nice and quiet. Pale late winter light filtered through the dirty windows of the Newsweek Building's top floor. I made friends with the Swan Song secretary, Fran, who was about twenty-five. She had big Italian hair and lived with her parents on Long Island. She liked her job, and told me the only band member who ever showed up at the office was Robert Plant, who granted an occasional interview in Danny's office. Fran and I ate tuna fish sandwiches for lunch while Danny worked the phones in his corner office. One afternoon, I watched Fran opening the day's fan mail. There were twenty-seven letters addressed, in often childish handwriting, to either Jimmy Page or Robert Plant at 444 Madison Avenue or in care of Atlantic Records at 1860 Broadway. (These mailing addresses were listed on Led Zeppelin's albums.) Fran methodically slit open and examined the fan mail envelopes, explaining that before the correspondence was thrown away, it was inspected for the occasional contraband— rolled joints, topless underage Polaroid snaps, Quaaludes—that Zeppelin fans tried to send the band. When she finished, she deposited the unread letters in her wastebasket. I asked if the band ever saw their fan mail, and she looked at me as if I was retarded. Later in the evening, after Fran had left for the day, and while Danny was talking to Steve Weiss about John Bonham's car registration problem in Dallas, I retrieved the discarded fan letters from the trash, barely a step ahead of the office janitor, and stashed them in my briefcase, resolving to examine this unrequited correspondence later.

Chapter 21

Letter from a Fan

It was still late winter in New York, and I froze in my boots as I walked uptown. I was looking forward to the warmth of the California sun as much as Led Zeppelin. I was also eager to read Zeppelin's fan mail.

I was staying in a big apartment, on Park Avenue at 86th Street, which belonged to my friend David. He was a photographer for the National Geographic Society, and so was often away. He was kind enough to make his enormous, inherited family flat available to me when I was in New York. There were sometimes others—relatives or friends—staying there as well when I was in town.

In this period, I was sharing the house with a Canadian ballerina named Claire. About twenty, very cute and blue-eyed, she had blown a recent audition with the national ballet and was now taking private lessons in the dance studios above Carnegie Hall in an attempt to advance her career. She was a nice girl, and fun to hang out with. We'd order take-out suppers from the Madison Deli and watch TV. I took her to see Charles Mingus's Jazz Workshop at the Village Vanguard. She also liked Led Zeppelin and played my *Physical Graffiti* records on the family stereo—*very* loud. She went to sleep at ten o'clock every night. "Sometimes," she earnestly told me, "one has to make sacrifices for the sake of one's art."

That evening, Claire was quite excited about the rescued Zeppelin fan mail and announced she would read all the letters. She picked one at random, addressed to Jimmy Page, 444 Madison Ave., NY, NY.

"Dear Jimmy," she read aloud. "*Wow!!!* I can *NOT* believe you are reading this. (I *hope* you are.) I am a *huge* Led Zeppelin fan, aged 15 and I am also 'into' black magic and playing guitar, so we have a lot in common. I am writing to tell you I had tickets to your concert in St. Louis that was canceled when Robert got sick. (*Boo!*) Then, when you came back later, I couldn't go because I had my 4-H heifer project due the next day. (We took second place. My heifer's name is Cheeseburger.)" This made Claire giggle. "Anyway, it would be real neat if you would *please* send me a signed photo by you and the rest of your band. And if you are ever in this part of Missouri, feel free to drop in any time. Keep rocking, your friend, Duane Fulkerson, Wentzville, Missouri."

The evening went on like that, until the willowy Claire retired to her room precisely at ten. I read the letters, some of them very long and confessional, until I fell asleep, just as Johnny Carson was signing off *The Tonight Show* at one in the morning. Tom Snyder was on next; his guest was Martin Mull. I slept through it.

◆ ◆ ◆

On Thursday evening, I came in from supper with friends. Claire, in a black leotard and pink tights, was eating a salad. Like most dancers, she had deformed feet. But with her long canary-colored hair tied back in a bun, in the soft light of the apartment, Claire looked like a Degas watercolor of a ballerina. "Your friend Danny has been trying to call you," she said. "It's about Led Zeppelin. He called three times, eh?"

Danny was still at the Swan Song office, and he picked up his private line at the first ring. "Jimmy is after me for the William Burroughs story," he said. "I found out that the article was written, and made the mistake of telling him. Now Jimmy is insisting I get a copy of the text. He's *quite* anxious about this."

Why is this a problem?

"Because the magazine is being pissy. The fucking editor won't give it up. Says it's against company policy, and Burroughs hasn't authorized it. Listen: Jimmy told me that his evening with Burroughs was one of the *high points of his life*—but *now,* he has this paranoid fear that he or the band will be mocked in the article."

That's really doubtful, I said.

"I know that, but Jimmy doesn't. He's got Peter [Grant] wound up about this now. Steve Weiss is calling me about it. *Gevalt!* We simply have to get a copy of Burroughs's piece."

What do you mean, "we"?

"*C'mon, man!* You *know* Burroughs. That's what you told me. I can't make any promises, but it wouldn't hurt your chances for some interview time with Jimmy if you showed up in Los Angeles with a copy of the Burroughs piece."

I see what you mean, Danny. I'll do what I can.

The next morning was Friday. We were leaving for Los Angeles on Sunday. Thus began a mad scramble to (somehow) score

William Burroughs's unpublished essay on Led Zeppelin. First, I called my friend Josh Feigenbaum, the *Crawdaddy* publisher. Josh didn't have a copy of the text, and affirmed that it was against company policy to show advance copies of articles. But Josh gave me Bill Burroughs's current phone number, and I called him at the loft on Franklin Street. I had met Burroughs in Tangier a few years before. A few months prior to this, I had conducted a long interview with him in Boston for a weekly paper, and we had gotten along well because we had a mutual friend in Brion Gysin, his great and frequent collaborator. Later, I'd heard Bill thought well of the interview when it was published.

Bill answered the phone. I told him I was writing about Led Zeppelin and was professionally curious about the article he had just written, and was there *any possible* way—"I know it's a lot to ask"—that I could read it?

"Read it? Sure, Steve. Why not?"

Bill explained that he didn't have a copy of the text, but he was sure that his assistant, James Grauerholz, who'd typed the final draft, had kept the original typescript. He gave me the number. I called James, who did indeed have the article, and I arranged to read the piece at his flat in the East Village.

James lived on St. Mark's Place, almost across the street from the tenements depicted on the jacket of *Physical Graffiti*. He was a tall young guy from Kansas, obviously devoted to Bill, and he handed me the manuscript of the Jimmy Page interview as he fielded calls relating to upcoming Burroughs readings and appearances.

I started reading. Titled "Rock Magic," the article was a rather dry journalistic account of Burroughs's visit to Zeppelin's concert at Madison Square Garden, and a summary of his evening with Jimmy Page. Fortunately, the phone rang again, and

James said that he had to leave—right away. I said I needed to finish reading the article. Maybe I could take it home and bring it back tomorrow? James said okay, and I was out of there. I ran to the Copy Cop shop around the corner on Second Avenue and made five copies of "Rock Magic."

The next day was Saturday. William Burroughs called me at noon and asked if I had his article. He didn't sound thrilled that I had somehow made off with his typescript. But I'd learned that serious reporting was often about deceit and manipulation. This unpublished Burroughs text would get me to Jimmy Page. I told Bill that I would get the pages back to him, right away, and he said to come to his loft at six o'clock that evening.

Which I did. Burroughs was cordial, offered me a drink, and put the pages in a drawer when I handed them to him. "I liked Jimmy Page," he said, "and I thought he was very bright. I suggested something like that rock music could be combined with older forms of trance [music] to produce a kind of . . . therapeutic response, in the audience, without the use of drugs or stimulants. With the power they [Led Zeppelin] have, their hold over their audience, maybe they could get some *real* magic going, instead of all that dry ice."

Burroughs swirled the ice in his whiskey. "I don't think I'd like to be in his shoes, though," he said, referring to Page. "Jimmy tells me there's some serious resentment building against the big rock stars in England now. You can feel it in the street, with people spitting on his Rolls in the King's Road. And Jagger and his wife are refused taxis in London when the older drivers see who they are. Last year, Mick was punched in the face by a customs agent in Paris. The rock stars are facing a lot of hostility. Many of the ones I've met seem rather . . . *lonely*, actually."

Back at 1040 Park Avenue, I telephoned Danny Goldberg.

"Danny, I've the Burroughs article! It's great! Jimmy will love it!"

"Way to go," he replied. "I'll call Jimmy right now and tell him you're bringing it to L.A. on Sunday."

CHAPTER 22

Abrupt Change
of Weather

An idling black Cadillac limousine was waiting for me outside 1040 Park Avenue on a frosty Sunday morning in
early March 1975. Danny Goldberg was in the backseat, tearing
through *The New York Times*, *Post*, *Daily News*, and the Long
Island paper *Newsday*. Already consumed were *The Village Voice*
and the *Soho Weekly News.* We rode out to JFK airport in cold
bright sunshine and silence, except for the rustle of broadsheet
and tabloid.

Waiting for us at the famous high moderne style TWA terminal were two other journalists who were going to California
with us, both on Led Zeppelin's tab (me, too). Tony Palmer was
a highly respected London writer who was covering Led Zeppelin for *The Observer*, the left-leaning English daily. Steven
Gaines was the editor of *Circus*, a teen-oriented rock monthly
published in New York that covered both the dinosaur bands

(Led Zepp, Stones, Elton John, Fleetwood Mac) and their reptilian younger brothers: Aerosmith, Peter Frampton, Thin Lizzy. We checked our luggage and went to the first-class lounge to wait for our flight.

I'd been up late at a jazz club (Bradley's, Jaki Bayard on piano) and was hungover and dissolute. By contrast, Tony Palmer—early forties, spectacles, thinning hair—was charming and convivial. He wore a smartly tailored brown velvet blazer with a tiny red rose embroidered in his left lapel. Steven Gaines—late twenties, expensive haircut, charismatic—was also well turned out in a hip leather jacket and green suede ankle boots. Steven looked very rock & roll, whereas I—late twenties, bad hair era, dressed down in old suede coat, faded denim, pathetic boat shoes—looked like a guy who worked in a used record store. Fortunately, Danny dressed more like me than like them.

Our seats were in the first-class cabin of a TWA 747. Before takeoff, the stewardesses brought us champagne and fresh orange juice—mimosas—which helped my hangover. Once in the clouds, they served a full breakfast—hot croissants, freshly scrambled eggs, good coffee: the works. I ate and chatted with Tony Palmer. He'd come up in the early days of the Beatles, and told me he wasn't a Zeppelin fanatic but had a lot of respect for Jimmy Page and the great success he'd achieved. I asked Tony what was going on in London now, and he spoke about the hot new bands emerging in a still-underground scene. These younger bands and their rabid, club-jamming fans were much younger, and they all claimed to utterly despise Led Zeppelin (and the Stones, and Elton) for being tax-exiled "boring old farts" who were out of touch with what was going on with 1975 teenage England—a place where the social contract was actually in some semblance of play and where "No Future" would become a rallying cry in days to come. (I think this was the first time I ever heard of the Sex Pistols.) Tony also observed that he didn't really think 1975 was Britain's finest hour. The country was in severe economic trouble, he said, and there was bound to be some kind of reaction from the kids. It was a shame that big-earning musicians like Zeppelin had to be tax exiles from their own country.

I asked Tony if he was promised interviews with the members of Led Zeppelin. He replied that he'd been guaranteed the usually garrulous Robert Plant, and probably (but not certainly) Jimmy Page. I thought his chances with Page were good. Danny had told me that one of his greatest publicity coups was getting a positive article about Led Zeppelin in London's *Financial Times*, which was read with tremendous pride by Robert Plant's accountant father, who had never approved of his son's choice of career. Led Zeppelin actually craved a measure of acceptance by the mainstream English newspapers, the ones read by their families, and so could be quite accommodating. Palmer asked about my assignment, and I told him that my one chance of getting face time with the elusive Jimmy Page involved payback for the William Burroughs manuscript that I had managed to acquire.

Tony: "Do you have it with you?"

Me: "Of course."

Tony: "Can I read it?"

Me: "Sorry. I'm sure you understand."

Tony: "No problem. Had to ask."

We both put our chairs back and went to sleep.

Danny was huddled in the first row of seats with Steven

Gaines because Danny needed to make sure that *Circus*, with its large teenage readership, was going to publicize Swan Song Records' other acts, and not just the insurgent, head-banging Bad Company but also Maggie Bell, the Pretty Things, and Mirabai.

Somewhere over Nebraska, the stewardesses served lunch: filet mignon, lobster tails, Côtes du Rhône. Ice cream sundaes and French cognac were then on offer. Then everyone in first class (except Danny) lit a cigarette for a postprandial smoke. It was a different world then.

The dulcet atmosphere of late winter Los Angeles was an immediate relief after the frigid rest of America. Another limousine waiting at LAX whisked the four of us, in light Sunday traffic, to the Continental Hyatt House at 8401 Sunset Boulevard, in West Hollywood. I was familiar with this establishment because I'd stayed there on an Elton John junket when I was with *Rolling Stone* in 1973. (The building had opened in 1963 as the Gene Autry Hotel, named after the singing cowboy who had built it.) Led Zepp had been lodging there since 1970. The band's antics were so outrageous—big color TVs hurled off balconies; feral teenage girls camping in the corridors with coolers and boom boxes; unmuffled motorcycles roaring down the hallways—that the locals renamed it the Riot House. On this leg of the tour, Led Zeppelin and entourage had originally been booked into the (boring) Beverly Wilshire Hotel, but that hotel's management had second thoughts after Who drummer Keith Moon had recently trashed his suite to the extent that vandalism charges were almost certainly being pressed.

Checking in to the Riot House, I was assigned to room 818. The walls were wine red. There were two large beds. Its open balcony offered a smoggy view of Hollywood's afternoon cityscape. I lit one of the dozen skinny joints I'd carried in my shirt pocket, put my feet up, and shut my eyes.

Twenty minutes later, as I was unpacking my clothes, the telephone rang. Danny was on the line.

"Can you come up right now? Jimmy wants to see you—*right away.*" The line went dead.

CHAPTER 23

The Pipes of Pan in L.A.

A year earlier, in 1974, I had spent several months living with a tribe of traditional musicians in the mountains of northern Morocco, recording their music for the National Geographic Society. The tribe had been "discovered" in 1950 by Brion Gysin, collaborator and friend of William Burroughs. I was following in the footsteps of the late Brian Jones, founder of the Rolling Stones, who, aided by Gysin, had first recorded the Master Musicians of Jajouka in 1968. After Brian Jones's untimely death a year later, the Rolling Stones had issued edited versions of his Moroccan tapes on their eponymous record label in 1971, and this record—*Brian Jones Presents the Pipes of Pan at Joujouka*—became the alpha product of the world music movement that began to flourish in the West a decade later.

Some other recent Jajouka recordings I was associated with had just been released on a small label, and I'd brought along a vinyl copy for Jimmy Page. This I grabbed, along with William

Burroughs's article, and tried to walk up the one flight to the floor occupied exclusively by Led Zeppelin. But the door to the ninth floor was locked from the inside. I walked back down and took the elevator.

Two big guys in casual clothes sat on chairs by the ninth-floor elevators, checking anyone who had business on the floor and sending everyone else downstairs. They directed me to the last door on the western corner of the hotel, facing Sunset. I knocked, and nothing happened for a long time. I knocked harder, and after a moment, the door opened with the chain on, and a pretty blond girl dressed only in bedclothes said, "Yes?" in a posh English accent.

I asked for Jimmy, and she said to go back and knock two doors down the hallway. The door closed in my face. The door she had indicated was blocked by a room service cart with a load of dishes and covered plates, which I wheeled aside. As I was about to knock, the door opened quickly and a haggard-looking Iggy Pop burst out and scuttled sideways down the hall like a land crab. Iggy had fronted the legendary Detroit band the Stooges and was now a ghostly fixture on the L.A. rock scene, as a sort of protégé of David Bowie. Then Danny came into the vestibule and motioned me into the darkened hotel suite, where *Burnin'*, the most recent album by the Wailers, was playing softly on the stereo.

It took my eyes a moment to adjust to the gloom, lit only by a dozen white candles, as Danny introduced me to Jimmy Page and tour manager Richard Cole, who began to open the curtains to let in a bit more light. Led Zeppelin's protean star guitarist was sunk into the sofa. He looked tired, with sunken eyes, and needed a shave. His long black hair was tousled. He was just waking up. He didn't stand up to shake hands. Before him was a low table and a collection of switchblades and ratchet knives. Richard Cole was tall, bearded, fierce, and offered me a glass of the Dom Pérignon champagne cooling in a silver bucket. As my eyes adjusted, I noticed a large stack of record albums and a pile of laundry in the corner. Two carts laden with covered room service dishes were off to one side. It was immediately clear that Jimmy had been sitting there for a long time. Danny told Jimmy that I had something for him, and I handed over the manila envelope containing "Rock Magic."

"How is it?" he asked in a high, scratchy voice. "Did you read it?"

I told him that I had liked the essay, and then explained how I'd gotten it; added that Bill Burroughs didn't know I was passing it along; and begged for discretion, because I wouldn't want the author of *The Naked Lunch* to be angry with me.

"Don't worry," Jimmy said. "You won't get any problems from us." As he spoke, his large hands fluttered in front of him. Then I handed Jimmy the Jajouka record. The colorful cover image of a traditional Moroccan musician in an embroidered robe caught his eye, and he perked up. "This a new Jajouka album?" he asked. "I about wore out my copy of the Brian Jones one. I'll have to listen to this later."

Trying to get something going, I mentioned that I'd been in Morocco recently and that some of the music on *Physical Graffiti* reminded me of things I'd heard in the streets of Tangier and Marrakesh. Jimmy sat up and clapped his hands. "I like hearing that," he said, and smiled. "Do you remember the names of the tracks that sounded like that?"

"Well, obviously 'Kashmir.' And then the one called—uh— 'In the Light.' The guitars sound like a Moroccan bagpipe band."

Jimmy smiled and said, "Yeah, right. Okay." And then, cryptically, "We're all about attitude, this band."

I didn't want to blatantly try to cash in on the Burroughs connection, at least not with Danny in the room. Jimmy sat back in the sofa and now seemed out of it, but I mumbled that I needed a few brief minutes of interview time with Jimmy, and it would be really cool if we could get together sometime, just for a very short moment or two. "Yeah . . . mmm . . . we'll try to get something together," Jimmy said, shooting a look at Danny. "There's a few I'm supposedly . . . *required* . . . to do." He paused and sighed. "I'm very *tired*, actually. We haven't been all that well—none of us has." The long lashes of his heavy eyelids came to rest, and Jimmy appeared to breath deeply. Richard Cole stood up. The audience was over. Then Jimmy came to, and thanked me for the article. "Can't wait to read it," he burbled.

Danny left the suite with me. "Nice try," he said. "I'll do what I can."

I asked what was going on with Iggy Pop, and Danny said he'd been trying to sell heroin to Jimmy. Then, when Jimmy demurred, Ig had offered a few bags to Danny. This annoyed Page, who scolded, "Come on, Jimmy! [Iggy's real name is James Osterburg.] Danny doesn't *do* that stuff. Get a hold on yourself, for fuck's sake."

Is Jimmy using heroin? He looks terrible.

"I don't know, to tell you the truth," Danny said. He laughed. "Better make that 'No comment' instead. C'mon, man—he's exhausted. He has a very hard time shutting down the energy he has to conjure for these performances. I do know that Jimmy can stay awake for several days with his guitar in his lap, just waiting for, as he says, something to come through."

Who was the blond girl who answered the other door?

"You knocked on that one first? That was Chrissie Wood, who ran off with Jimmy before the tour started. He's also got his girlfriend Lori stashed in a room on another floor, and he might be flying in Bebe Buell for these L.A. shows, although I kind of doubt it. Of course you won't print any of this, or mention it to the other writers.

"We're playing San Diego tomorrow. Jimmy's doing a couple of interviews for me in the afternoon. They're taking the plane, so the limos leave the hotel around five o'clock for the airport. Yes, you're on the plane. I'll let you know the timing in the morning, so be ready to go. See you later—God bless."

CHAPTER 24

The Loud Drummer

The Riot House actually seemed more like the Quiet House. Late on a Sunday afternoon, the marble lobby was deserted except for an almost invisible John Paul Jones collecting his phone messages at the front desk. Last time Led Zeppelin had been in town, the lobby was besieged by crazy teens from Hollywood and the San Fernando Valley. Now the only signs that Led Zeppelin was in residence were three black limos and a gold stretch Lincoln parked in the hotel's drive. Across the street, facing the hotel, loomed a giant Sunset Strip billboard for *Physical Graffiti*. The bar off the lobby was empty except for two guys in leather and shades who looked like they worked the promotional end of the record business.

Robert Plant, I'd learned, wasn't even staying at the hotel, preferring the company of a girlfriend who had a country cottage in the far reaches of Malibu Canyon, about an hour north along the Pacific Coast Highway.

I rang up Peter Simon, who was hanging out in L.A. while his sister Carly was helping her husband, James Taylor, make an album in Hollywood. Peter said he was still interested in shooting pictures of Led Zeppelin for my magazine article, so we arranged to meet for supper at The Source, the *haut*-Hollywood health food restaurant near Tower Records on Sunset Boulevard.

Later, over brown rice and tofu (Peter and his real good-lookin' girlfriend, Nancy Dix, were vegetarians), I explained that there was no room on the plane to San Diego for him tomorrow night but that Danny had promised him full backstage access at the following two shows at the Long Beach Arena, later in the week. Peter was more of a Deadhead than a hard-rock fan, but he said he'd be happy to tag along as long as nothing bad happened, considering the Led Zeppelin's sleazy reputation. We finished our insipid herbal teas and arranged to meet at the Riot House the following day.

There were a few harmless kids in blue denim and short skirts hanging around the lobby. The bar was vacant, so I called it a night and went to my room. In days of yore, it had been Zeppelin's rowdy young road crew that had wreaked the most havoc in the hotels, but at the Riot House, there was not a stoned long-hair in a tour shirt anywhere in sight. Past experience had taught me that if band members were using drugs, the roadies were often using as well, since they were usually a crucial conduit for dope on the road. And most people in a heroin glaze were less than interested in throwing a heavy hotel TV off a balcony.

It had been a long day, one that had started in frigid New York. I stepped onto my balcony and stood for a moment in the dark, smoggy atmosphere of the Los Angeles basin. The only sound was the traffic on Sunset Boulevard. The millions of lights below stretched out into Hollywood until they disappeared into the dark haze. Upstairs, Jimmy Page was probably still sitting with his guitar in his guarded, candlelit suite. Robert Plant was probably listening to coyotes howling in a Southern California canyon. John Paul Jones . . . who knew? I didn't want to know what John Bonham was up to. I took a blissful hot shower and prepared for a long, restful sleep.

The earthquake happened at about three in the morning. (I'd been dreaming about Peggy Day.) First the walls started to shake, and then my bed began to vibrate. I sat up amid a thunderous rumble that was truly terrifying. Was this it? Was this The Big One? I turned on the light and saw the mirror over the desk shaking in its frame. Then the noise and shaking stopped. Abruptly it began again. I ran to the balcony, but the city seemed asleep despite the catastrophe. What the hell was going on?

I realized suddenly that I was not experiencing The Big One. I—and every other sleeper in the Riot House—was listening to music, played at the loudest possible volume on serious speakers, one floor above mine.

Being a jazz fan, I recognized the music after a few moments. Alphonse Mouzon was the loudest, hardest-hitting drummer in the jazz world—bar none. But he also swung, and was currently the top drummer in the business. I'd seen him play several times, and always had to sit in the back of the club because he played so loud. His employers had included McCoy Tyner (who had worked with the powerful drummer Elvin Jones in John Coltrane's quartet), Miles Davis, Weather Report, and most recently guitarist Larry Coryell's fusion band, Eleventh House. Mouzon also made his own albums for the Blue Note label, the most recent of which—aptly titled *Mind Transplant*—

was being played directly above my head at torture-level volume. I was familiar with the recording, and knew we were almost to the end of the first side.

When the music finished, I called the front desk, which explained that the hotel was aware of the problem but that the guest involved was neither answering his phone nor responding to the night manager's knock. "Unfortunately, sir, we are not able to give out the identity of this guest, but we're of course trying to contact him." Just then the needle fell into the groove and began side two of *Mind Transplant*. Within a minute, my room started to shake again. The faux Monet water lilies on the wall were vibrating. That's when I realized what was happening.

My room was directly underneath John Bonham's suite, and he had set up a drum kit and was playing along to Alphonse Mouzon's rhythms, which could be described as an extremely swinging fusillade. It was brilliant, the whole thing, because Bonham also had that ability to get you on the dance floor and then pulverize you with rim shots and artfully dropped bombs. I decided that this was part of the trip, so just try to enjoy it. Here was John Bonham showing me his favorite musical influence. I sat there in my vibrating bed and listened to the loudest drummer in rock play along to the loudest drummer in jazz. It was almost funny.

When the music stopped, I turned off the light and rolled over. But no! Bonzo had just dropped the needle onto Alphonse Mouzon's 1973 album *Funky Snakefoot*. So I ended up pushing PLAY on my Sony TCS-310 cassette machine and making an archival but muffled recording of the night's unwanted entertainment with the Sony's less-than-optimal, built-in condenser microphones.

Mercifully, there was no more post-midnight Led Zeppelin drum practice once the first side of *Funky Snakefoot* had faded out. The Continental Riot House itself seemed to breath a sigh of relief, and fell back into an uneasy sleep, an hour shy of dawn.

CHAPTER 25

A Spiraling Vortex

Led Zeppelin went back on the road at five o'clock on Monday, March 10, 1975. The lobby of the Riot House was now more accurately the hotel's nickname. Roadies scurried around. Security held a bunch of teenagers at bay in the driveway, where six stretch limousines laid in wait. Entourage members—the young doctor with his medical valises, various girls and women, journalists and the photographer—waited for the elevator doors to open.

Robert was first out, chatting with an L.A.-via-Colorado cowboy-style cocaine dealer (from central casting; he even carried the stuff in an antique beaded Hopi peyote pouch) who was also trying to sell Robert the extra-classic 1955 Chevrolet sedan parked in front of the limos. John Paul Jones was next (almost anonymous), followed by John Bonham, who looked queasy, and tense around the darting eyes. The doctor went over to Bonham, and they exchanged a few words. Apparently, John Bonham—

worthy constituent of Alphonse Mouzon—felt sick, and the pressure was on him to play great every night in California.

Finally, Jimmy Page wobbled out of the elevator, accompanied by the two FBI agents and Richard Cole. A longtime teenage fan, whose presence in the lobby was tolerated by the band, rushed up and shouted, *"Jimmy, you are so far out!"* Page stopped and asked, "Do you mean . . . that I'm a *spiraling vortex?*"

And there was Peter Grant swaggering from the bar with two beautiful companions, an ungentle giant in a gaudy, swashbuckling costume, and he was ready to go. There was a shout from kids on the street when they saw Robert's yellow locks, and he waved to them as if he were the lord of the castle and they were the peasants waiting across the moat. Now Cole expertly matched entourage member to limo ("slutmobile" in his parlance). The band was given the majestic Mercedes-Benz Pullman 600 with six doors, a crystal bar service, and smoked glass. Grant, the lawyer, the lawyer's girlfriend, and two women who were keeping Grant company were seated in a seriously vulgar, gold-painted Lincoln Continental stretch limo. (Attorney Weiss—and I could hardly believe this—had accessorized his hip business attire with a ludicrous purple velvet pimp's fedora.) Danny, his media entourage, the tour doc, the blow merchant, and various (quite attractive) sluts crammed into the remaining cars, and we were off to the airport. Richard Cole had decided to take the Starship for a twenty-minute ride to San Diego, which would have taken three hours by road.

But, just a few blocks down Sunset Boulevard, the band's limo suddenly lurched into a gas station. What was this? John Bonham emerged and disappeared into the toilet. He came out after a few moments, smiling wanly, looking sheepish. Back on the road, the convoy cruised south on Sepulveda Boulevard, until the band's car veered off into another gas station, and again Bonzo staggered into the toilet. The doctor got out, knocked on the door, and was told to fuck off. Indeed, the doctor's stature was nearing its bottom. He'd never been forgiven for Robert's long recovery from the flu, early in the tour. Cole hated him and in New York had grabbed the doctor by the neck in a drunken moment while throwing him into a car, which drew the wrath of Peter Grant. Now, at the Riot House, underage girls had been seen leaving the doctor's room late at night, and the hotel detectives complained to Zeppelin's security team. (The doctor himself would later complain that Jimmy had pilfered Quaaludes and other tranquilizers from his medical bags while he was away from his room.)

Almost at the entrance to LAX's private aviation gates, the band's limo pulled over again, and Bonzo dashed into a Burger King for more relief. It turned out that he was suffering from horrible belly cramps and diarrhea. Mouzon's Revenge, I thought to myself.

The sky was darkening and it began to rain. The limo convoy pulled right up to the Starship's mobile staircase, and the band boarded first, greeted by the two smiling flight attendants. Led Zeppelin had been the first band to charter the new Starship in 1973, and except for a few untoward incidents, relations were good between band, pilots, and crew. The big runic LED ZEPPELIN logo was painted on the fuselage (replacing the vivid stars and stripes from Elton John's earlier *Rock of the Westies* tour). Once inside the customized Boeing 720B (officially called Starship One), I got a chance to inspect most of the plane before we had to fasten our seat belts.

The entire interior cabin was carpeted in deep purple shag. The front section had a few booths and swiveling leather chairs.

Amidships were a brass-covered bar and a seating area comprised of three large sofas and more leather seats. A state-of-the-art video player—still a rarity in 1975—could show an impressive library of VHS tapes: Looney Tunes, the Marx Brothers, *Deep Throat*, and *Behind the Green Door*. A built-in organ stood near an impressive pop art target painting at the end of the bar. Farther aft was a cozy private lounge (with a working electric fireplace) and more sofas. The bedroom was in the tail, occupied almost exclusively by Jimmy and Peter Grant, and off-limits to everyone else. The bedroom décor was Vegas honeymoon. A huge fake-fur rug covered a king-sized waterbed. The private shower was reputed to have been the portal for several rock stars' entrance into the fabled Mile-High Club.

The Starship took off in a serious thunderstorm. Lightning flashed as the big jet lumbered down the runway. Once aloft, the pilot, operating under safety rules different from commercial aircraft, banked and weaved around the thunderheads, causing drinks to spill. I noticed some fellow passengers tightening seat belts and glancing nervously out the windows.

When the Starship finally leveled off, things quieted down. I was sitting near the front with the other writers. John Bonham was in a booth near the forward bulkhead. He seemed in a sort of stupor. Suddenly, he looked up and growled my name. "Stephen Davis, eh?" This got my attention, and my blood ran cold for a second. The Beast had crushed that Atlantic Records promo guy's glasses on this plane. The Beast had to be pulled off one of the stews. How did he know me? But then someone brought him a drink and his beastly attentions were diverted elsewhere. I resumed breathing.

There was a huge flash of lightning, and the Starship shuddered and dropped a thousand feet. Someone screamed, "Air pocket!" This was greeted with uneasy laughter.

I moved to the bar area and sat near Robert Plant, who was holding court for the pretty girls on the plane, most wearing floppy silk pantsuits and stacked heels. These were later identified as "the roadies' girlfriends." Hovering near Robert was Nick Kent, the correspondent for London music paper *New Musical Express*. Kent was decked out in high pop fashion: shaggy hair, mucky face, Edwardian jacket, lace shirt, checkered trousers, absurdly stacked-heel boots. Kent had written a pissy review of the Zeppelin's New York shows, which had caused him grief a few days earlier at a party in Los Angeles also attended by John Bonham and Richard Cole, who had poured their Bloody Marys on him and told Nick Kent that his life wasn't worth shit. Kent had been invited aboard the Starship to make up for this, but he was obviously stressed and was sticking close to Plant and Page and the hippie coke dealer they were hanging with.

Just then, the door to the aft bedroom opened and Peter Grant emerged, heading toward the bar. (Grant was reportedly still upset about the recent Florida cancellation, which had guaranteed Led Zeppelin half a million dollars for a single show.) The big figure sported a blue silk kimono top over his gigantic gut. A maroon tango hat with blue plumes completed the picture of a hard-living rock & roll pirate about to attack and plunder a hospital ship. Massive chunks of turquoise and silver bracelets adorned his enormous wrists. His sausage-looking fingers bristled with more Navajo finery. As Grant ordered drinks from the bar, Robert leaned over and observed that if anyone was the *real* "last of the ravers," it had to be Led Zeppelin's gangster manager.

The Starship now descended amid tremendous blasts of lightning. I could feel the landing gear going down. The plane's sound system was playing Elvis Presley's classic "Teddy Bear." The plane shook, sickeningly, in the turbulence, but Robert Plant stayed cool. He remarked that if the Zeppelin was going down, the Elvis sound track was totally appropriate since Elvis was where Led Zeppelin had come from.

The plane was diving now in the storm. I looked at Danny Goldberg, and he looked at me. We both laughed. The whole thing was so gonzo. Rain lashed at the windows. Robert got up and peered out over the wing. "Aha! Dear God," he yelled. *"We're landing in a supermarket!"*

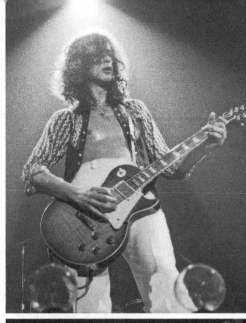

PAGE

CHAPTER 26

Dionysus in San Diego

As the Starship taxied over to the terminal, six limousines pulled up to the steps and popped open their trunks. The band got off first; as Jimmy Page walked forward, he stopped by us writers and was introduced to Steven Gaines by Danny. "Same limo as me?" he asked a surprised Gaines, who duly followed Page into his car. The other writers felt like rejects. The band was astonished to see a little group of fans huddled in the rain by the private aviation gate, flashing their cameras at the wet cars as they sped by. People thought rock stars led strange lives, but what about the fans?

The limo convoy splashed over to the San Diego Sports Arena and discharged its passengers into Led Zeppelin's dressing room, actually just a locker room, which was already a cauldron of milling people with backstage passes pasted to their clothes. I walked over to a table that had a coffee service, and Robert asked me to make him a cup of tea with lemon and plenty of honey. The band changed into stage clothes as promo guys from the record company tried to arrange introductions to the local radio heavies and their wide-eyed children. Robert, having doffed his jeans, stood bare-legged in his briefs as he shook the hand of an unbelieving girl who was too overcome to speak. Bonzo was pulling on his white boiler suit, derby hat, and low-cut sneakers. I was amazed to see, heaped in the corners, piles of gifts from the fans. There were boxes of fresh fruit, a barrel of fried chicken, crates of citrus and grapes—the luscious bounty of Southern California—and at least a hundred floral bouquets, all completely ignored by the band.

Amid the chaos of the locker room, the doctor suggested that John Bonham lose the one-piece boiler suit, which would be hard to disrobe if an emergency toilet run was necessary during the concert. These next few California shows would be the only ones in the tour that saw the drummer playing in his street clothes.

It was close to showtime, so the band (and Nick Kent) followed the cocaine cowboy into the shower room to do lines away in private. When Led Zeppelin came out, they put on the craziest rock concert I ever witnessed.

I watched from the side of the stage with Danny and Tony Palmer. The sold-out crowd of teenagers squirmed in their chairs until the lights dimmed, and then they let out an ecstatic roar when Led Zeppelin took the stage. It was like tigers let out of the cage as John Bonham played the pile-driving drum intro to "Rock and Roll." As the band blasted off in an explosion of light, the kids got up and surged toward the stage, flattening every chair on the floor. Girls up front were squashed against the fences and pulled over the wire barriers by the anxious security squad to save them from the crowd. I saw two bloody fights in front of the stage during "Rock and Roll," and then a short but vicious brawl between some bikers and security staff during "Over the Hills and Far Away."

Robert sarcastically congratulated San Diego on its torrential English weather. He repeatedly asked the rabid kids to ease the dangerous crush down front, which formed weird tidal surges of young humans in front of the stage. Sitting at his keyboards for the midsection of the concert ("No Quarter," "Kashmir," and "Trampled Under Foot"), Jones expertly worked the bass pedals with his feet as he played the spooky jazz, Carnatic vamps, and up-tempo electro-funk of the three songs. The audience went into an orgasmic swoon merely at the sight of Jimmy Page strapping on the red Gibson double-neck guitar, preparing to perform the hallowed "Stairway to Heaven."

The highlight of the show was the encore, "Whole Lotta Love," with Bonzo playing the most barbarous and reverberant drums I'd heard on this tour. The kids responded with more ravenous infantry tactics. Then about a dozen teenage girls were hoisted onto their boyfriends' shoulders as the song went into its final Neanderthal crunch. A girl near the stage took off her T-shirt, another her halter top, and soon half the elevated girls were wiggling bare breasts at Robert as he promised them every inch of his love, deep down inside. This provoked a mad stampede backstage, as the road crew fell over themselves to get a look at young naked bosoms. The Led Zeppelin show turned into ten minutes of bawdiness and fun from the darkest depths of Mordor. More people fainted. Some disappeared underfoot or were passed through to the hardworking security shirts. Jimmy shifted down into "The Crunge," and then into "Black Dog," and suddenly they were gone. The white-hot L E D Z E P P E L I N sign, throbbing behind the drums, was for a few moments the only light in the big hall. The audience fired their lighters and begged for more, but we were already being chucked into the limos by General Cole and then sped to the airport in the worsening monsoon conditions.

The Starship was the last plane to lift off before San Diego closed the airport because of the weather. The exhausted band disappeared into the aft cabins, and the usual cocktails and buffet were canceled by the pilot so the stewardesses could stay in their seats as the jet bucked and banked in the storm. It was much more turbulent in the air now. The entourage was quiet, nodding out or chewing their nails. I sat next to flight attendant Susie, who told me that the Starship was owned by former sixties teen idol Bobby Sherman and Ward Sylvester, who had produced *The Monkees* TV show. They'd bought the plane, used, from United Airlines for $600,000, and spent another quarter million outfitting it as what Richard Cole described as "a fucking flying gin palace." Top-grossing rock bands, and the corporations that loved them, leased the Starship for $2,500 per flight hour; so a typical journey, say New York to Miami, cost about $11,000. She said this was no problem for the Starship's regular passengers. The 1975 tour was Zeppelin's second lease. Other rockers Susie had flown with included Elton John, Deep Purple, and John Lennon. She liked John Paul Jones because he actually played the plane's organ. (A favorite seemed to be "I've Got a Lovely Bunch of Coconuts.") Susie was also excited because she'd heard that the Rolling Stones had booked the Starship for two months in the summer of 1975, and she'd always wanted to meet Mick Jagger.

As the Starship began to descend into LAX, Susie confided that Richard Cole had several dozen cases of Dom Pérignon champagne stored in the airplane's hold. "I think it's all '64 and

'66," she added knowingly. "Only the best for our passengers, right?"

Back at the Riot House, there was a mad dash for the bar at midnight. Everyone who'd survived the turbulent flight of the Starship felt lucky to be alive. The exhausted musicians were out of sight. For them, it was another of those nights when there was no wild party. I just hoped Bonzo was going to let me get some sleep.

Chapter 27

The Prairie Princess

The following night (Tuesday, March 9), six limos again lined up in the Riot House's drive, along with the '55 Chevrolet and a large red truck-mounted camper. Again, rain was pelting down. The rumor buzzed that John Bonham still had the runs, hence the camper with its private toilet. Finally, after a delay, the drummer walked unsteadily from the elevator and was directly ushered into the camper with Robert and their two minders.

Cole then loaded the limousines, except for one stray girl who was left on the curb. She was different from the other sluts hanging around the tour. First, she was very attractive, with long auburn hair, and she wore no makeup. Second, she wore an ankle-length prairie-looking dress, red-and-white checkered, except that the back was scooped way down to the base of her spine, so it was obvious she was braless. Her skin was snow white and flawless. She looked like Miss Nebraska, only more wholesome. No one knew her. She had just turned up at the evening slutmobile selection. She seemed annoyed at not getting a ride to the show with the band. What was she doing here?

But wait. Richard Cole evidently changed his mind, because he now motioned her into the car he was riding in, and with that the convoy was off to the Long Beach Arena, normally about an hour away. It took two hours because of the rain and rush-hour traffic.

Led Zeppelin went onstage more than an hour late. "Good evening, Long Beach," Robert said after the third song. "We apologize for the slight delay, but we didn't have any tickets." He told the audience that the band was enjoying the English weather they were having. "If you want to sit still, forget it."

The greasy, saturnine opening notes of "In My Time of Dying" now drew applause. The audiences were becoming familiar with the long jam from repeated encounters with *Physical Graffiti*. The interaction between Jimmy Page and John Bonham was uncanny, pointillistic, and obscenely alive. The metallic jangle of "The Song Remains the Same" drew a frenzied roar from the crowd, but Page's twelve-string guitar was way out of tune. Robert apologized for this. "The Rain Song" then stunned the kids into a stupor, and Jones finished them off with a soporific electric keyboard solo that ventured into the most banal clichés of the cocktail lounge pianist, while the band left the stage. I was sitting in the tenth row. Five minutes into Jones's solo, everyone around me who could still walk went to the bathroom. I went backstage, got a bottle of beer, came back to my seat, and Jones was still soloing. Eventually, he played for more than twenty minutes, and killed the show.

After that, the sound system started to fail. There were twenty-six microphones onstage, twelve on the drums alone. A hundred eighty speakers could deliver 120 decibels of rock thunder, and things were bound to go wrong despite the subsequent rage of Peter Grant. Soon the sound techs and roadies began crawling around the stage, trying to stop the keyboard amps from buzzing. There was a loud banging noise coming from behind the drums after "Kashmir," and Robert told the audience that someone was building a henhouse backstage. "No," yelled Bonham. "They're building a fucking shithouse!"

The rest of the show was boring and subpar. Robert Plant, usually the ever-preening shagging master, seemed subdued, and he missed the high notes in "Stairway" ("Is there a *LADY* we all know . . ."). I was so bored I started studying the band's expensive new lighting effects. The effects were so out of character for previously propless LZ that the British writers were describing the production as Zeppelin's "American show." According to Danny's press release from nearly three months ago, 172 colored lights were mounted on a horseshoe-shaped truss held up by twenty-eight towers. Three supernatural laser beams were activated from behind the drums as Jimmy began the main guitar solo of "Dazed and Confused," supplying a dash of science fiction to the poisoned atmosphere of the long piece. The lasers pulsed and quavered when Jimmy drew his violin bow and began to scratch the guitar strings, lending an aura of practical magic to an ancient incantation.

Jimmy Page saved the evening in the encores. Wielding the golden Les Paul guitar at just below crotch level—you could only do this if you were six feet tall and had long arms—he tore into "Whole Lotta Love," cut with "The Crunge," and then sent everyone home singing "Hey, hey, Mama . . ."

The band did a runner after that. I was in the second limo after the band car and soon noticed that the convoy was being shadowed by teenagers in fast cars—GTOs and Firebirds—who were easing up to the speeding limos at 75 mph so their girlfriends could try to see the band up close. Despite the rain, the girls rolled down their windows and were yelling stuff at the band's car up front. The situation was dangerous, considering the speed and the slick freeway, but the intrusion stopped once the cars turned off the highway. (The following night, there was a police escort from Long Beach.)

Back at the Riot House, the band disappeared into their suites. Danny Goldberg remarked that despite everything one ever heard about the insane Zeppelin tours, this Tuesday night was more typical than not: no parties, no excess, no Rainbow. Peter Grant, for instance, liked to get his folded laundry back from the hotel and iron his own shirts in his suite.

Jimmy Page lit candles, sat with his knives and guitars, and tried to turn off his adrenaline tap. Robert Plant was driven up the coast to his girlfriend's house. John Paul Jones called home, a country house in the shires, where his wife was just making breakfast for their two daughters before they were off to school. John Bonham blacked out, and was put to bed.

In the bar was the pretty young prairie princess who'd gotten a ride to the show earlier in the evening. She'd sat near me during the concert, and I'd seen her staring at Robert Plant with a gaze that bordered on transfixed, religious adoration. Now she had a demure shawl around her shoulders and was nursing a glass of wine with Peter Grant's two girlfriends. I wanted to speak with her—there was a story here—but it seemed uncool to approach her without an introduction. So I went to my room, had a smoke on the balcony, left the sliding door open so I could hear the hissing of the traffic on wet Sunset Boulevard, and turned off the light.

CHAPTER 28

The Golden God

The next day was Wednesday, March 12. The warm California sun was shining silver over the greening Hollywood Hills. Ace photographer Peter Simon arrived after lunch with his cameras and a thermos full of chai: milky sweet Indian tea flavored with cardamom, prepared by his sexy, laid-back girlfriend, Nancy Dix, to sustain him through his ordeal with Led Zeppelin, shameless purveyors of Myth Metal and Freak Folk. Pete also brought some star-quality Panama Red, which we were smoking on my balcony when the phone rang.

"Stephen, it's Danny. Can you come down to my room as quickly as possible? Thanks. God bless."

Danny had a small suite on the third floor. I let myself in, and he motioned to the bedroom, where Robert Plant was lying like a young king on a king-sized bed. He was dressed in tight jeans, snakeskin boots, and a seriously tie-dyed shirt. He looked at me and said, "Ah, the one that didn't smile."

What do you mean, I asked.

"On the plane the other night," he said, "you never smiled once."

That was probably true, I replied, but I don't really like to fly and there was that storm and a certain amount of stress.

"You're right," he said. "Let's press on." Danny suggested doing our interview right then and there, but I said that my photographer was upstairs where the light was better, and besides, he had a thermos of freshly made chai.

"Chai?" Robert leaped up. "Let's have some chai. My wife's Indian, you know." Robert, carrying the *The Harder They Come* movie sound track album, followed me up the concrete staircase to my room. He complimented the yellow Moroccan slippers I was wearing, and when I asked about the record, he said he was going to have *The Harder They Come* played over the sound system before Led Zeppelin went on in Long Beach tonight.

I introduced Robert Plant to Peter Simon and they made a sort of hippie-brother connection. Robert was seriously interested in the hot chai. As I handed him the cup, he earnestly inquired, "There's not any acid, or anything, in this, is there?"

No acid, I said, and offered him some of the Panama Red.

"No, thanks," he said. "Actually, I gave up cocaine . . . this morning. A very destructive substance when abused. It's just tea with lemon for me from now on. Well, maybe some chai, too. This is good, man." This was accompanied by an ironic little smile. I didn't believe a word of it.

There was a knock on the door as Robert and I sat down at the table by the window to record our talk. Peter let in a young girl, about seventeen, very pretty and dark skinned, with dark, curly, luxurious black hair. She was dressed as an Indian princess, with a dime-store warbonnet of colorful feathers, a little fringed buckskin skirt, and her long legs tucked into beaded moccasins. "Hi, Lori," Robert said. "Want to listen in?" And to me, "She's an old chum."

We started in on reggae. I told him I'd recently interviewed Bob Marley and Perry Henzell, who'd directed *The Harder They Come*, the cult movie that put Jamaican music on the map. He said he and Jimmy had just been on the island of Dominica, where the local Rastafarians had treated them to ganja and some sort of hallucinogenic "jelly fruit."

Robert had been doing interviews, and people kept asking him about the band's supposed affinity with black magic— their legend had them making a deal with Satan to ensure their success—and now it seemed Robert wanted to get something across.

"All that magical stuff," he began in his high, husky speaking voice, "and of course the music, might well get the audience high, but I *never* allow myself that luxury, and I don't think Jimmy does either. On the other hand, Jimmy'll tell you that sometimes he goes into trances with the audience, and I believe him. But that's not where I'm coming from. I've always got to be in control, or the party's over pretty quick. What I live for are the King Arthur moments when the music and the vibe just brings everything into a communion. That's what gets me off."

We spoke a bit about *Physical Graffiti*, still reigning over the charts at number one, and I asked Robert about "Kashmir."

"It was originally called 'Driving to Kashmir,'" he said. "I spent some time in India after we formed the group, and that's been a major influence on my life. I learned a lot about a different kind of music, with different kinds of scales and singing styles. And I remember being in one of the towns, recording street musicians, when a Pakastani plane flew over to bomb and there was a sudden blackout. Everything stopped except the street musicians, probably because they thought they weren't gonna get paid. Anyway, all the bombs missed the town and landed in the fields. So I think the musicians might have played the danger away, so to speak. If their music could protect the town, I'd like to think we could have a force like that. Just kind of . . . playing the danger away."

Did he, I asked, actually make it as far as the Vale of Kashmir?

"No, not yet," Robert laughed. "Our Kashmir is really a state of mind. But in a way, we go there every night [on tour]."

I said I'd seen a bunch of the concerts now, and that "Stairway to Heaven" seemed to provide the greatest spiritual lift to the kids. I asked where his inspiration for the bustle in the hedgerow and the lady buying the stairway came from.

"I wrote those words one day after reading a great book called *The Magic Arts in Celtic Britain* by [antiquarian] Lewis Spence. Jimmy had the music going in the other room, and I went off to make some notes, and the words came to me, at one sitting, as if I were being guided to write down what I did. So maybe there was a force. And I think about that a lot. It's no longer my absolute favorite Led Zeppelin song, but sometimes I feel that if we didn't have it, we could possibly be just another group heading over the hill."

I asked about direct musical influences. "Elvis," Robert answered immediately. "Elvis singing 'Little Sister.' Little Richard doing 'Tutti Frutti.' Robert Johnson doing 'Traveling Riverside Blues.' Sometimes I tell the audience that 'Trampled Under Foot' is our version of Robert Johnson's song. Then there's Blind Willie Johnson's 'In My Time of Dying.' I guess Bob Dylan liked it, too.

Bukka White doing 'Shake 'Em On Down.' Howlin' Wolf. Muddy. And I loved the San Francisco bands—the Airplane, Moby Grape, especially Spirit. All great stuff."

What about Jimmy? "With him, it was everybody I just said, and then you throw in the guitar players: John Fahey, Davey Graham, John Renbourn. When I first went to Jimmy's house, I was shocked because he had the same records as me, only a lot more of them."

Peter Simon was shooting (future iconic) black-and-white pictures of Robert during our conversation, the motor drive of his Nikon camera caught on the tape I made of the interview. It had been cloudy for a while, but when the sun came out, Peter asked Robert to step out on the balcony so he could be photographed overlooking the big *Physical Graffiti* billboard opposite the hotel. When I opened the sliding door, Robert stepped onto the balcony, stretched his hands out over the smoggy Hollywood vista, shook out his long blond locks, and shouted, *"I'M A GOLDEN GOD!"*

Peter framed and shot this scene, and I had to laugh because, indeed, at that shining moment with this charming rock star who was charging toward Valhalla while singing of Vikings and hobbits and a lady who shines white light, it seemed that the golden god thing could actually be true.

"I'M A GOLDEN GOD!"

LZ ROADIE MAGNET, PLANT, AND THE AUTHOR

CHAPTER 29

Access All Areas

fter an hour, Robert's roadie knocked on the door to remind him it was ten minutes to limo call for the second Long Beach concert. Lori had disappeared during the interview. I hadn't noticed her departure, because the twenty-seven-year-old Robert Plant's very presence in the room was so intense. Peter and I rode down in the elevator with Robert and the roadie. Flashbulbs popped at Robert as we walked out to the cars. He got in the driver's seat of the '55 Chevrolet along with the roadie, Jimmy Page, and the cocaine salesman, and took off for Long Beach, followed by Bonzo in his red camper, as it began to rain again. Peter and I were directed to the last limousine in the line, along with Danny and Steven Gaines. There were too many girls this evening, and Richard Cole was doing triage with as much civility as possible under fire. A stubborn girl rejected for the second limo (too much makeup) snuck into our car and introduced herself as Desiree, but Cole saw this and nodded to a security goon, who asked her to leave. She got out, slammed the door, and stormed back into the Riot House. Now only the mysterious prairie princess remained on the curb, again in a long, backless dress, except that tonight the check was blue instead of red. But the cars were now full, and she was left standing there, looking more annoyed than humiliated. It was, I thought, the price she'd paid for not being a slut.

Danny asked how the interview with Robert had gone, and I said it had been interesting to spend an hour with a golden god. Danny sighed and said he'd heard that line before. I asked about Lori. "That's Lori Maddox," he said. "She was Jimmy's girlfriend when she was fourteen, which was only about three years ago. They had to hide her on the plane as they moved around the country. Since then, Jimmy's moved on, but she's like a mascot, and they all like her, so she's always around when the band is in town. Now, believe me, Lori is a legend along Sunset Strip."

I asked Steven Gaines of *Circus* magazine about his limo ride with Jimmy Page in San Diego two nights ago. Gaines said that Jimmy had wanted a quiet word with him because *Circus* had published a paperback biography titled *Robert Plant*, and Jimmy wanted to discourage him from publishing one with the title *Jimmy Page*.

The rain got heavy on the 405 freeway, and traffic stood still for at least half an hour. At the Long Beach Arena, the scene in the dressing room was another madhouse. I went to make tea for Robert, but his roadie beat me to it. In a corner were more fan gifts: enormous melons, more fruit, more flowers. Danny had arranged "Access All Areas" passes for Peter and me, so before the show, I slipped out of the dressing room, wandered down a corridor, followed an arrow, and soon found myself on Led Zeppelin's stage as it was being readied for the show. Mick Hinton, Bonzo's roadie, was standing by the big Ludwig drum kit in his white boiler suit. He seemed approachable, so I asked if I could get a closer look. "No problem, mate," he said. "Just don't even fucking *think* of touching anything."

I asked if he would sort of give me "the tour."

"Well, mate, I'm not really supposed to talk to ... *journalists*," he said with obvious distaste. "But, seeing as 'ow you've got a stage pass and all, I suppose I can show you his kit."

The numinous Ludwig drum set, "Orange, Transparent," Hinton pointed out as I took notes, centered on the 26-inch bass drum, augmented by a 14-inch ride tom-tom, a 16-inch floor tom-tom, and an 18-inch floor tom-tom. The 14-inch snare drum, like all the others, was nailed to the stage floor.

As with the Ludwig firm, Bonham had an endorsement deal with the Paiste company for his cymbals. Hinton pointed out the 24-inch ride cymbal, the 18-inch ride, the 16-inch crash cymbal, and the pair of 15-inch Sound Edge hi-hats. John liked these, Hinton advised, because their serrated edges gave the cymbals a "cleaner" sound.

Behind the kit was a 38-inch Paiste symphonic gong, a 29-inch Ludwig machine head tympani, and a 30-inch Ludwig pedal tympani. These last three instruments comprised the battery used in Led Zeppelin's take-no-prisoners encores.

What about the drumsticks?

"Fucking *trees*," Hinton answered. "Ludwig 24s. Hickory wood. Biggest they make. It's all fucking all right *there* in the sticks, innit?"

Thank you, Mick Hinton.

After a few lines of Peruvian marching powder, Led Zeppelin took the stage and crashed into "Rock and Roll." The Long Beach Arena erupted into a cauldron of volcanic magma. The audience was so porno that the kids up front almost melted into the band. Deadhead Peter Simon, shooting pictures from the side of the stage, more used to jam band mellowness, looked at the scene and said, "This is . . . *totally wild*. I've never seen, like, this *sexual frenzy* before." Led Zeppelin was at its 1975 apex now, hard as nails, down and dirty, and only a few thousand people ever heard it—the real deal.

Jimmy Page was wearing his new outfit, a black silk stage suit embroidered with exquisite, scaly Chinese dragons down the legs, the dragon an exclusive symbol of the emperor himself only, and further garnished with spangled stars and crescent moons. A massive chunk of turquoise in a silver setting hung around his neck. The shoes were black loafers with white tongues. Page's look was cosmic Nudie suit, Zen-style rockabilly, and extremely cool, I thought.

"The vibes are better tonight," Robert told the customers after "Over the Hills."

He apologized for the long delay, citing treacherous conditions on the roads. He claimed it was snowing in Hollywood. "Better vibes than *last* night, anyway. Too many reds [barbiturates] or something." He introduced "In My Time of Dying" as "as an old work song—long before Mr. Zimmerman [Bob Dylan] heard it." After this induced a malarial fever in the becalmed audience, Led Zeppelin ripped into "The Song Remains the Same," which lifted off okay but exploded when Jimmy broke a guitar string. Robert stopped the show: "Hold it! Hang on! What the f—" The roadies scrambled, and while the Les Paul was repaired, Robert said, "They didn't tell me it was like this in Valhalla." He also said it was the first string to break onstage in Zeppelin's almost seven-year history.

John Paul Jones played more meandering, lounge-lizard "jazz" during "No Quarter," prompting Plant to compare him to

boring American TV crooner Andy Williams. (This was actually fairly insulting.) Later, Robert introduced Jones as "Mr. Liberace." (Jones's keyboard music *was* pretty corny stuff, so there
was a certain honest hostility in Plant's onstage comments.)
"Trampled" was introduced as "Trampled Under Jimmy's Foot,"
reportedly because Plant hadn't been allowed to play his reggae
record over the PA before the show, supposedly because they
were running so late. After "Stairway"—interrupted by Robert's
rhetorical query, "Does anyone remember laughter?"—he told
the crowd that Led Zeppelin was finally playing like itself again,
after a hard road of travails, and by next week, when they were
playing three nights at the L.A. Forum, "we should be . . . what?
Sky high!"

The encore now changed a little. Robert dedicated "Whole
Lotta Love" to attorney Steve Weiss on his birthday, and Led
Zeppelin shook the Long Beach Arena to its basement. Grungy,
stomping "Heartbreaker" closed the show, the lightbulbs flashed
on, and the band and entourage ran for the limos. Police outrid-
ers kept the kids away from the cars as Led Zeppelin sped back
to the shelter of the Riot House in the cold rain.

Chapter 30

The Application of Attitude

ack at the Riot House, we said good night to Peter Simon, who'd shot six rolls of film between the Robert Plant interview and the Long Beach concert. I told him to thank soulful Nancy Dix for that invaluable pot of chai that had lured Robert Plant upstairs. Danny invited me to join him at a birthday party for Steve Weiss, which was being thrown by his girlfriend. The party suite was half full of Zeppelin entourage and L.A. friends when we got there around midnight. The lights were low, and the atmosphere subdued. I'd heard that Weiss was involved in the various controversies over Jimi Hendrix's estate after Hendrix died in London five years earlier, but I wasn't about to bring up the subject.

I hadn't had time to eat after our interview with Robert. I drank a gin and tonic, and another, when I spied John Paul Jones standing in a corner with a drink in his hand. I asked Danny to introduce us, and chatted with the truculent but polite Jones for a few minutes. He asked who I was writing for, and I said *The Atlantic*. He seemed confused and turned to Danny, who explained it was a famous old literary magazine that was trying to get hip. Oh, Jones said, and turned away to inspect the canapés. I had a mad notion to ask him about the founding legend of Led Zeppelin, which held that magic-obsessed Jimmy Page convinced the other guys in the New Yardbirds to sell their souls to Satan in return for the usual success and riches. According to the story, which Robert supposedly related in late 1968, a magical spell was drawn up, and Jimmy, Robert, and Bonzo (both nineteen years old) signed the paper in blood. John Paul Jones, the story went, didn't sign this blood oath. This story began to spread from New York and Los Angeles groupie cliques during Led Zeppelin's first tour in 1969, and never really went away. Led Zeppelin's instant success—biggest band in the world within three years—gave the legend credibility in the eyes of the credulous.

As I was screwing up my courage with another drink, a birthday cake appeared, and a refreshed Peter Grant came in with a bottle of Dom Pérignon in each large paw. Richard Cole joined the party a few moments later.

"Where's Pagey, then?" Grant asked him.

"Sitting in the bar downstairs."

"Who's with him?"

"Phil Carson and some cunt from the press."

This was my cue. As glasses were raised, I slipped out of the party and headed for the bar, now almost empty at one o'clock in the morning. Jimmy was at a table in back with two men. I sat at the next table and waved to Jimmy, who nodded back. Phil Carson worked for Atlantic Records in London, and Jimmy looked to be giving an interview since the second guy was tap-ing. After a few minutes, that conversation ended and the second man left. So I introduced myself to Phil Carson and asked Jimmy if I could buy them a drink and get a few quick quotes for my article while we were there.

Page said he was very tired, but sure, make it quick. I asked him a few questions, hoping I didn't sound drunk after four cocktails, and tried to scribble shorthand notes on the bar napkins. My first question, about technique, was quickly dismissed. "It's never a question of technique," he said. "I just deal in emotions."

Well, emotions, then.

"It's even simpler than that," he said. "It's really about . . . attitude, isn't it? The application of attitude. It's either there, or it isn't."

What about the magic thing?

"Magic is a system of will, and of strength. That's what interests me about magic. I can't produce material magic, *real* magic, so what we offer is the illusion of magic—mechanical devices that perform illusions while we play music. And in my own mind, the difference between the illusion, and the reality, of the lasers, and the theremin, and all that is . . . hazy. What's a laser beam? Magic, isn't it?"

Richard Cole now came into the bar and looked at me darkly. Jimmy and I both got up, shakily. Time to go upstairs. I held out my hand, and he shook it gently. He looked really exhausted. I asked, "How long are you going to do this?"

"Nothing lasts forever," he said over his shoulder. "I'm going to enjoy it while I can."

Quite a day, I thought, as I rode up the elevator. I'd done the two crucial interviews I needed for my article. No one cared about John Paul Jones, and I was afraid of the drummer, whose

Alphonse Mouzon records I could now hear blasting from the floor above me as I walked down the carpeted hall to my room. I'd attended the best Led Zeppelin concert on the tour so far, and partied with the entourage. I could go home now if I wanted to, but I decided to stay until Danny told me to get lost. He'd told me that Led Zeppelin's shows in L.A. were always the best because they were playing for their friends, colleagues, groupies, movie stars, and the heavies of the record business.

Alcohol wasn't really my thing, and the cocktails and no supper were having an effect. Getting my clothes off was difficult, and the walls were rubber. Then someone knocked on the door. I swam over and opened it to find the prairie princess, looking as fresh as clover with her blue-checked dress partly covered by a knitted shawl with Plains Indian markings. I thought she was a hallucination.

"Yes?" I managed.

"Is Robert here?" Her voice was soft, like wind through wheat.

"Robert? Plant?"

"I was told he was in this room."

"Who said that?"

"A man downstairs." She looked past me and saw that I was alone.

"Would you like to . . . um, come in?"

"Sure," she said, and brushed past me, making slight body contact. She smelled like sage grass. I closed the door. She sat down where Robert had sat ten hours earlier. When I told her this, she took a deep breath.

"Who are you, anyway?" she asked, taking off her high heels.

I told her about my job. She told me she was Ann Miller, or something like that. She said she was a second-grade teacher from Zionsville, Indiana, and she was twenty-three years old. No makeup. No pretense—an American girl to die for. She said she was a rabid Led Zeppelin fan, and specifically an aspiring Robert Plant groupie. When she heard Robert was going to be in Los Angeles while her school was on spring break, she decided to drive to L.A. and meet him somehow. What would happen after that, she didn't know, but just getting to spend some time with him would be okay. She knew where the band might hang out in L.A. because she was an avid reader of *Hit Parader, Creem,* and *Circus.* She had a cheap room on a low floor facing the hill-side for a few nights in the Riot House, but she didn't even think Robert was staying there. Then she ran out of money. But the garage attendant took pity on her and let her sleep in her car. She was so pretty and wholesome that soon other hotel employ-ees were slipping her leftover food from the kitchen and the room service carts. The staff told Ann there were lots of girls like her, since many well-publicized bands stayed at the Riot House. The reason she'd knocked on my door was that the night bellman knew that Robert had been seen going into my room that afternoon.

I told her about my interview with him. Ann yawned. I asked if she wanted to have a sleepover date—better than the car, and besides, it was raining and cold—and she just laughed. Then she got up and pulled the spread off the unused bed. She stepped out of her long dress—her breasts were perfect—and slipped under the blankets. She turned on her side and pulled the covers up to her ears. When I came out of the shower a few minutes later, the lights were off. I could hear her breathing in her sleep. I got in my own bed and spun around in my head until I, too, was in the arms of Morpheus.

When I woke up at noon, she was gone. She'd even made the bed.

CHAPTER 31

Tomorrow Will Be Too Late

The next afternoon, Danny invited me to his suite downstairs for breakfast, and I was just sitting down to the Riot House's famous smoked salmon omelette and a pot of coffee when the phone rang. The front desk was calling to say that a girl was in the lobby demanding to see Jimmy Page. She had told the clerk that Mr. Page's life was in danger and that she had urgent information for him. Mr. Grant and Mr. Cole were not answering their phones. Could Mr. Goldberg have a word with her? Danny said to send her upstairs to his room, and sorry for any trouble.

She looked about twenty-five, and she appeared in a long maroon cloak with a hooded cowl. She had a mousy little face, pinched with stress. Her brown hair was dry straw. I looked at her and thought: She's in a hippie cult. Children of God? The Process? Manson family? (Love the cloak.) Danny introduced himself as a vice president of Swan Song Records, but she wouldn't shake his hand or say her name. When she began to speak, a nervous tic caused her eyes to blink rapidly.

She said she was an emissary, but wouldn't say who had sent her. She had to see Jimmy Page, she insisted, because someone had foreseen something evil in his immediate future. The thought was that the "bad energy" could happen the following night in San Diego. "What sort of bad energy?" Danny asked. The girl stammered that her warnings were personal to Jimmy Page only. She knew Page was in this hotel, and she needed to see him right away because, she swore, the last time the person who sent her had foreseen something evil, someone was shot to death in the street—before her eyes.

Danny took all this in. I was totally creeped out. Calmly, Danny assured this apparition that Jimmy Page was resting from three straight concert nights, and not even he, Danny, could see Jimmy until the following night. At this the girl got a frantic look. Her eyes misted with tears, but she held it together and didn't cry.

"Tomorrow night will probably be too late," she whispered.

After a few more minutes, Danny persuaded her to write a note to Jimmy, which he assured her that he would deliver himself. Hyatt House stationery was produced, and the girl—left-handed—scratched about twenty lines and then seemed to draw some symbols at the bottom of the page. She folded this into an envelope and sealed it with her tongue. She seemed unwilling to leave, but Danny again assured her it was impossible to see Jimmy Page. She was furious, and slammed the door on her way out.

My eggs were cold now. Danny took the envelope containing her message into his bedroom and burned it, unread, while he invoked the black goddess Kali and Sai Baba, the reputed miracle worker of Puttaparthi. When the ashes cooled, they were spread before an image of Lord Krishna. Danny said he would have to report this threat to Peter Grant, who would probably add another layer of security in San Diego on Friday night.

That would have been the end of the story had not Squeaky Fromme—one of Charlie Manson's girls—pointed a loaded pistol at President Gerald Ford six months later in Sacramento from about two feet away. A Secret Service agent grabbed the gun before she could fire. It turned out there was no bullet in the chamber, although the clip was full. I was shocked when I saw her on the evening news because I thought it was the same girl who demanded to see Jimmy Page at the Riot House. I was almost sure of it. I called Danny, of course, and he said it looked just like her, but he couldn't be sure. Later it was reported that the would-be assassin just wanted to be reunited with Manson family members serving life sentences for the seven murders they committed in 1969. But a federal judge sentenced Squeaky Fromme to life and sent her to West Virginia, as far from California's prisons as possible. We never found out if it was our girl or not. (I believe it was.)

This was a Led Zeppelin day off, and it had stopped raining. The sky was leaden and the air was dry. I went down to the garage to see if I could find Ann Miller or whatever she was called. She'd said that she was driving a Buick Roadmaster, but I'd been so out of it the night before that I couldn't be sure. Both garage levels were empty of big station wagons bearing Indiana plates. I found the Mexican attendant smoking a joint behind a Dumpster and asked about the girl in the checkered dress. He sadly informed me that she'd left at dawn.

By now, I thought, Ann Miller would probably be in Arizona,

charging east at top speed to Indiana, heading back to her class-room of seven-year-olds. I'd bet money there was an eight-track tape of *Physical Graffiti* blasting out of the dashboard. At least she'd gotten to the Led Zepp concert in Long Beach. It was something to remember.

The Riot House garage proved to hold other surprises. Peter Grant's two girlfriends, who'd been in residence for at least ten days, were pulling up stakes. But their old Pontiac wouldn't start. The ladies had the hood up and were staring at the engine in puzzlement, pulling at cigarettes.

Some loud rock music from KLOS was roaring up from the floor below. I walked down and checked out a Corvette, its radio blasting. The driver was also revving the engine occasionally. Closer inspection revealed that John Bonham was sitting in the driver's seat. Next to him was Mick Ralphs, from Bad Company. Steve Weiss had been unable to register the 'Vette (which had been trucked over from Texas) in California on short notice, so Bonzo (according to the Mexican guy) was spending hours in the garage, sitting in the car and gunning the engine just to hear it vroom. A few days later, he bought a Model T Ford and had both cars shipped to his place, Old Hyde Farm, in Worcestershire.

The Riot House's garage held even more wonders. Sounds of conflict now arose, and, one floor above, two Led Zeppelin road-ies were beating up a kid they'd caught trying to break into Bon-zo's intestinal-problem camper. (They'd been sleeping in the vehicle at the time of the attempted crime.) This quickly became a bloody affray as the kid was no water lily and fought back. Hotel security arrived quickly, and the malefactor was subdued. As the West Hollywood sheriff's deputies led the hapless burglar away, the two ladies roared out of the garage, tires squealing, having finally gotten the Pontiac started.

CHAPTER 32

Little Sister

t was Thursday, and an off night for Led Zeppelin. I invited
Danny to supper, but he had other media to attend to. I met
some friends at Dar Maghreb, a chic Moroccan restaurant in
Hollywood. Some rich Arab had spent seriously on the décor,
but the food was basic couscous, tagine, and pigeon pie. We had
drinks in the bar and then moved to a table. I looked around the
room. Michelle Phillips—stunning—with a party of four. Robbie
Robertson and Martin Scorsese and their wives. Members of
the English band Foghat. Off in the far corner, at a table under a
canopy, sat Jimmy Page, Joe Walsh, and their dates. Later, as I
was leaving the gents, Jimmy was coming in through the out
door. "Spying on me, eh?" he rasped.

I said I was off duty, so not to worry.

Back at the Riot House, there was a note to call Danny. He
asked if I had enough material for my story, and I said that
indeed I did. He said my room at the Riot House was good until

Saturday, and after that, I was on my own. He recommended I see Led Zepp's shows at the Forum if I possibly could, and that he would try to help with tickets, but demand was enormous and there would be no more stage passes for Peter Simon and me. I thanked Danny and said that he and his employers had already been more than generous to us. I told him that I'd even review Mirabai's album for *Rolling Stone* when it came out.

Later that night, the bar of the Riot House was quiet but for some well-dressed women from the travel agents' convention that was taking over the hotel for the weekend, and a couple of Zeppelin roadies enjoying a nightcap. I sat nearby and we nodded—they knew who I was—and I offered to buy them a drink. Then we had another. Both were about thirty or so, and the older one had been with the band from the early days. The other was on his second American tour. They were both from around Birmingham and had Midlands accents. They were classic English roadies—good, dependable guys. They wanted to know what other bands I'd worked with, and I told them that hanging out with Bob Marley and the Wailers was about the most fun I'd ever had. I was getting tired, and moved to pay the bill, when the younger roadie surprised me with "Don't you want to ask *us* any questions?"

Sure, I said, waking up. Let's do an interview. I'll get my tape.

No tape, the older one said. No notebook, neither.

Okay. First question: What about the story that Led Zeppelin did a deal with Satan?

Bollocks, said the younger roadie.

Erm, the older one mumbled. Not so fast. We heard about *something*, back then. Two of 'em were very green, never been away from 'ome. Could be something to it. Dunno, really.

Second question: Did Led Zeppelin really stuff a dead shark into a groupie at that hotel in Seattle?

That happened, the second roadie said. Fucking Frank Zappa wrote a song about it, didn't he?

I was in the room, the older one said. It happened, but not like one 'ears it. First, it wasn't a shark. Next, she was rarin' to go. Next, it was Richard what did it. Next, everyone was so drunk they were falling over.

Third question: There seems to be a lot of heroin around this tour. True?

They looked at each other and smirked. The older one said, We dunno nothing about that sort of thing, do we?

Tell 'im about what you were saying earlier, the young one said to his mate. About Robert and that song.

Oh, I . . . dunno.

Go on.

I ordered another round.

Well, don't say where you 'eard this, right? But you know that song, "What Is and What Should Never Be?"

Sure, I said. It's my favorite song on *Led Zeppelin II*.

Well, don't say I said so, but what *was*, and what *never* should have been, was the fact that young Percy was seein' his wife's little sister, on the side, if you know what I mean.

This was delivered with a pop-eyed incredulity that made me laugh. I asked the older roadie how he knew this.

We *all* bloody knew about it, because 'e would bring the sister to the rehearsals, and during the breaks, the two of 'em'd be off in the fucking corner, fooling around. And the little girl was maybe sixteen years old—at most. And they *told* him, fucking Percy, they said, you're fucking *mad*. But he would just laugh and carry on. A right little minx she was, too. And that's what

PLANT

that song just happens to be about. "It's to a castle I will take you"—bloody hell. What a larf.

Great story, I said.

Don't quote me, he replied. And by the way, if you want confirmation, get your hands on a copy of *Physical Graffiti* and listen to "Black Country Woman." See for yourself. It's all right there, innit?

I had the cassettes in my room upstairs. I put headphones on and fast-forwarded to almost the end of side four. "Black Country Woman" was the penultimate track. (The Black Country was an old name for the English Midlands, left over from mining and industrial times. Early in his career, Robert Plant was billed as "The Wild Man of the Blues from the Black Country.") As the tape rolls, Jimmy is playing guitar, Jones the mandolin. After the plane goes over and Jimmy says to leave it in, Robert croons, "Hey, hey, Mama, what's the matter here?" to a bouncy, old-timey string jam. His old lady is giving him a hard time, causing him disgrace, throwing beer in his face. It's a song about marital strife. "But that's all right," he confides to his wife. "I know your sister—too." Then he pleads to know why she treats him so mean, why she's making a scene, and then taunts her again in a soft, cooing voice. "But that's all right, I *know* your sister, too." As the song grinds to a halt, Robert whispers into the microphone, "What's the matter with *you*, Mama?"

Well, that's pretty blatant, I thought. I wondered what Maureen Plant, Anglo-Indian Black Country woman, made of this. And then I realized that perhaps the song could only have made it onto *Physical Graffiti* if Robert was fairly certain that his wife never listened to his songs on Led Zeppelin's records.

CHAPTER 33

Cherry Bombs and Toilet Paper

riday, March 14. Led Zeppelin was playing in San Diego that night and then leaving town for a three-show tour of the Pacific Northwest. The crew was scurrying around the hotel all day in preparation for the decampment from Los Angeles. I noticed Bonzo's red camper being towed out of the garage and assumed his ailment was cured.

Peter Simon came over with contact sheets—prints of his negatives—from the other night, and several of his photographs of Robert Plant relaxing in my hotel room proved to be some of the best ever taken of him. Peter shot some frames of Danny and me eating a room service breakfast, and that was the end of his involvement in our little project. I walked him to his car, and he told me that he'd been in touch with Peggy Day. She wouldn't mind hearing from me, if I felt like it. She was living with some people in Carpentaria, a surf town south of Santa Barbara. Peter gave me her number.

I called right away, but she wasn't in and I left a message. I thought about it. She was someone I loved but couldn't be with. But she was a friend and very dear to me, and all the intensity and passion of the Led Zeppelin music I'd been experiencing, live, every night, mitigated against caution. When the phone rang an hour later, I was so glad to hear her voice, I had to laugh at myself. She gave me the address, and I said I'd see her the next afternoon. She promised me a picnic on the beach.

Danny wasn't going to San Diego, where a second show had been added to the tour after the first had sold out in half an hour. I wasn't supposed to go either, but on my way back from the car rental agency on Sunset, I happened to be in front of the hotel during the five o'clock limo call for that night's Led Zeppelin show. There were only four limos in the hotel drive, this being a low-entourage show. Nevertheless, Cole pointed me toward the last barge in the convoy, which I shared with the doctor and several charming, well-dressed, heavily perfumed young ladies wearing lots of kohl and eye shadow. On the way to the airport, it started to rain.

This was a charmed evening in that I was, for a moment, automatically accepted as a part of the tour. The Starship was waiting for us, and once aloft I chatted with the Scottish comedian Billy Connolly, who was then mostly unknown in America but played an annual circuit of Scots pubs and nightclubs on both coasts and Chicago, where his bawdy humor reduced his homesick countrymen to toilet water. He'd been staying at the Riot House while working in L.A. and had been invited aboard the Starship by Richard Cole, who'd run into him in the hotel bar. The weather was dirty, and again there was lightning to starboard. Connolly winced every time the plane lurched. By now I was a Starship veteran. John Paul Jones played backgammon with someone I hadn't seen before. John Bonham was literally belted in his seat, held in check by minders. Plant and Page were out of sight in the back. The hostesses were practicing making tequila sunrise cocktails in anticipation of Keith Richards's command of the Starship that summer. The girls made one for me. It was too sweet.

Led Zeppelin was on fire in San Diego, where the audience was again rampant and violent. Strings of exploding firecrackers flew onstage, and cherry bombs burst near Jimmy and Robert up front. It got really crazy for a while when one teenage terrorist down front threw a series of cherry bombs—tiny gunpowder grenades—toward Jimmy during "Trampled Under Foot." Then this person got involved in a fight and was dragged away by security in an ugly scene. I wondered if this was the bad energy the Mansonoid girl from the day before had warned of. John Bonham's Jurassic "Moby Dick" solo lasted for what seemed like eons, boosting beer sales and bathroom flushes in that part of San Diego. I didn't think much of John Paul Jones as a piano player, but it was at this show that I realized he was so crucial to what Page and Bonham were doing that he was clearly indispensable. No other bassist could play that hard with those two. Without Jones, it would have been a different band. During the bow solo of "Dazed and Confused," a spiraling roll of toilet paper that was flung from the scrum of sweaty young fans missed Jimmy Page's head by an inch. Led Zeppelin's second encore was again the lusty "Heartbreaker," followed by a runner to the limos and a mercifully calm Starship ride back to LAX.

The next morning, I packed up and went downstairs to say good-bye to Danny, who was flying back to New York. My friend had given me what turned out to be a precious opportunity to observe Led Zeppelin almost from within, with access that few people got for an extended period. I told Danny I hoped my article lived up to the faith he had in my work.

Then I checked out of the Riot House, drove a rented Buick Special down winding Sunset Boulevard, turned right up the Pacific Coast Highway, and hugged the coastline for two hours until I got to Carpentaria. She was waiting for me in front of a funky house in a crowded neighborhood near the beach. We held each other tight for a few moments and then broke apart, saying how cool it was to see each other again.

She grabbed a wicker basket and a Mexican blanket and we set off for the beach, just a few blocks away. The light was blindingly white, but when we walked over the dune, the whole thing turned ocean blue. She was barefoot, wearing jeans and an embroidered shirt, and she looked like a California girl: healthy, honey blond, tanned, freckled, clear-eyed. She picked a spot where we could watch the surfers riding lazy midday waves, and spread her blanket. Lunch was sandwiches and salad and two bottles of Dos Equis beer—very cold.

I told her about my adventures with Led Zeppelin, and answered her questions about people on Martha's Vineyard that we knew. We didn't talk about the previous summer, since there wasn't much to say. She said she had been living in this quiet beach town with friends for about six months and was going back to school in September to get her degree so she could teach art in the school system. She worked, part-time, in a used book store in town, and gave me a copy of *The Sheltering Sky* by Paul Bowles, which she said I might enjoy.

I'd never seen her look more beautiful.

She had a boyfriend who was interested in her, she said, someone from a well-off family back East. She said she would like to come back someday, and have children and a house of her own. After that, we didn't speak much, just sat and looked out to sea.

As the sun began to turn red toward the western horizon, I told her that I thought about her a lot and that I was sorry for any hurt I had caused her, but that our time together had been an experience I would never forget. She said it meant a lot to her, to hear that.

I walked her back to the place where she lived, and thanked her for the picnic. We hugged, and I drove back the way I'd come in the beautiful, soft Pacific twilight. We hadn't even kissed. I never saw Peggy Day again.

CHAPTER 34

A Town of Great Fishermen

n Sunday the Starship took off from Los Angeles and flew north. Led Zeppelin passed over San Francisco without landing, which was odd since, from the band's earliest days, the city had been one of Zeppelin's biggest markets. But on its last tour, Peter Grant had upset the status quo of the concert business, in which touring bands generally split the box office 50/50 with the local promoter. But by 1973, Led Zeppelin was so big that Peter Grant announced that his band would take 90 percent, leaving the pathetic remnant for the local promoter. The concert industry howled, but Grant advised them that 10 percent of Led Zeppelin's business was better than 50 percent of nothing. The promoters caved, and the other big bands followed suit. Grant met stiff resistance only in San Francisco, where promoter Bill Graham had a near monopoly on the concert business and an ego as big as Grant's. Danny told me that it was like King Kong versus Godzilla when these two titans of the rock industry negotiated. On this leg of the 1975 tour, Graham apparently made so many demands that they couldn't reach an agreement, with the result that the Starship landed in the rain at Sea-Tac Airport, and Seattle got two sold-out concerts instead of one. (I heard later that Peter had promised Bill Graham two big outdoor concerts in the Bay Area when the Zeppelin returned to America for more concerts that summer.)

Led Zeppelin checked into the Edgewater Hotel, located on Pier 67 near downtown Seattle. It was a favorite haunt of touring bands because guests could rent rods and reels and fish in Elliott Bay from their hotel rooms. This was also the place where Led Zeppelin's reputation reached its early nadir after it was reported that a groupie had been penetrated with a newly dead shark that had been reeled in by John Bonham. (Frank Zappa had indeed written a song about this called "The Mud Shark" for his band, the Mothers of Invention.) On its first visit, back in 1969, the band also amused itself by hurling their color TVs into the bay. When Peter Grant went to pay the bill, the hotel's manager remarked that he'd always wanted to throw a TV into the bay himself. "Have one on us," Grant famously roared, peeling off another five-hundred-dollar bill from the enormous roll he carried. The manager went right upstairs and dumped the TV off the balcony of the presidential suite.

There was, of course, no mayhem in Seattle on this tour. In fact, the hotel manager told Grant that a convention of Young Methodists had outdone all previous touring bands in thoroughly trashing the Edgewater a year earlier. They even tore up the carpeting in the corridors and threw it into the bay.

People who attended Led Zeppelin's four concerts in Seattle and Vancouver over the next week, or wrote about them, or who have studied the various bootleg recordings made of them, all agree that these were the finest shows the band played in 1975. After two months on the road, the band was finally performing to what sounded like its true creative capacity.

The week began on Monday, March 17, 1975, at Seattle Center Coliseum. A teenage fan showed up at the stage door with a gift for Jimmy Page: an incredibly rare, early model Les Paul guitar in pristine condition—and obviously stolen. Jimmy received the kid and accepted the guitar. The valuable instrument looked like one of Jimmy's that had been stolen from Led Zeppelin's van, in Seattle, in 1970. The kid was given tickets to the concert and shown the door. Someone in the entourage arranged to have the guitar quietly shipped to England before anyone caught on.

That night, "Rock and Roll" was performed with an adrenalized aggression that felt like a floored Cadillac rushing downhill, hands off the wheel, and the audience knew they were in for a special night. "Good evening," Robert said after the third song. He noted that the show had started on time, a first for Led Zeppelin. "It's more than a pleasure to be back in this seaside town," he continued, tongue in cheek. "That is right. Ha-ha. A town of great fishermen—including our drummer." This drew laughter, for the shark episode was common knowledge in Seattle, where the FM radio DJs had been laughing about it for weeks in the run-up to Zeppelin's appearances. The encores got longer now, as Jimmy Page began to really get into playing the guitar, improvising more every night and seemingly obsessed with the theremin's outer planetary broadcasts during "Whole Lotta Love."

Two days later, the Starship flew to Vancouver, British Columbia, where Led Zeppelin checked into the Hyatt Regency. At Pacific Coliseum on March 19, they played one of the longest shows of the tour. "Kashmir" was dedicated by Robert Plant to "our tour manager, Richard Cole, an upright British subject."

This dedication was indeed a tribute to Cole's competence, professionalism, and taste in vintage champagne. This night's performance of "Kashmir" was a cosmic odyssey, an exotic journey constructed by Page and Bonham to build to a symphonic crescendo that brought the audience to its feet. Years later, Robert Plant would call Jimmy Page "the Mahler of the electric guitar." Recordings taped that night in Vancouver bears this out.

After playing some light rhythms with brushes on Jones's lengthy "No Quarter," John Bonham was introduced to Seattle as "the king of jazz." He played "Moby Dick" for twenty-two minutes while his bandmates disappeared. When he finally thundered to a stop, Bonzo received the usual standing ovation and lighter display. "Thanks, John," said Robert afterward. "And—by the way—the blow job in the dressing room was *fantastic*."

The encores were dedicated to Peter Grant, whom Robert acknowledged had made it all happen for Led Zeppelin. "He's the one that gives us the blow jobs in the dressing room." Page proceeded to extemporize "Dazed and Confused" for almost forty minutes, interrupting the flow from bombast to "Woodstock" with an extended foray into a guitar transcription of a J. S. Bach cello étude. This then morphed into faux soul brother funk—"The Crunge"—and finished with "Black Dog."

Led Zeppelin had bombed when they last played Vancouver, two years before. The show had been described in the press as inept and lame, and Robert had collapsed two hours into it, so there were no encores. Robert acknowledged this when they played the coliseum again on Thursday, March 20. "Something weird happened to me that evening. The light show was amazing, and I wondered what the name of the group was." John Paul Jones played his "No Quarter" lounge keyboards for half an hour. Robert introduced Bonzo as a rotten, stinking pig. During

"Whole Lotta Love," Jimmy Page, with flame-colored Chinese dragons running down the legs of his trousers, seemed to be using the radio waves of the antique theremin to communicate with spirits of the dead.

The Starship flew back to Seattle the next morning. They were back at the coliseum that evening (Friday, March 21), again starting almost on time. Led Zepp was feeling well now, after five weeks away from home, and the band was growing back into its scaly self. "Rock and Roll" dominated, and the Seattle fans went crazy. Halfway through the show, Jimmy indicated that he wanted to play some blues music, so Robert announced a pause and a set change after "Trampled," apologizing to the drummer ("Sorry about that, John") for the unexpected, long, and passionate rendition of "Since I've Been Loving You" that followed.

After "Moby Dick," the Seattle fans beheld an unusual scene of chaos on the stage. "Dazed and Confused" was supposed to start, but Jimmy Page was seen shouting and cursing at someone in the wings to his left. Robert, playing for time, asked the crowd if they were having fun. Meanwhile, a furious Page looked like he was about to heave his guitar at someone in the wings. "Ah, erm— it seems that Mister Page is having a fit," Robert told the kids while Bonzo played a little rhythm to keep things going. Eventually, the show resumed, and earned multiple ovations, after which the Zeppelin rode back to its hangar at the Edgewater Hotel.

It later turned out that there were two possible reasons for Jimmy's wrath that evening. First, a brief but nasty fight had broken out in the wings between a backstage intruder and the road crew during "Moby Dick." And also, the criminally sourced, museum-quality Les Paul guitar that the anonymous kid had laid on Jimmy turned out to have been stolen from a local high school music teacher by an ex-student. Page was pretty sure this was the instrument that had disappeared in Seattle years before. The police arrested the kid and managed to track the guitar to the airport as it was about to be shipped to Page's house in London.

Jimmy Page got clear of the problem, but he was reportedly mad as hell.

CHAPTER 35

Transmitter of the Gods

Monday, March 21. I decided that even though I was ex-entourage, I needed to see as many of the three Led Zeppelin concerts in Los Angeles as I could get into. I moved onto a friend's living room sofa in Century City, and that afternoon, I drove over to the Riot House to see what was happening. The lobby was indeed jammed with girls, road crew, most of Bad Company and Pretty Things, and assorted hangers-on. I sadly noted that the backstage passes had changed from yellow to red for these shows. I had my yellow pass in my pocket. From the bar, I watched Richard Cole load the swollen limo convoy and take off for the Los Angeles Forum, located in the city's Inglewood section.

I followed in the Buick and parked nearby. Just to see what would happen, I put on my outdated pass and walked around back to the stage door. The guard was talking to two girls and didn't even look at me. I took off the outdated pass and tried to look normal. Ahmet Ertegun, president of Atlantic Records, walked by in conversation with Mick Jagger. I nodded to my old Boston acquaintance J. J. Jackson, the black FM rock disc jockey who, in a simple twist of fate, had introduced Led Zeppelin at those Boston Tea Party shows six years earlier. Now he was working at L.A. powerhouse KLOS and would again introduce Led Zeppelin tonight at the Fabulous Forum, as the arena billed itself. (In 1982, Jackson would become one of MTV's first VJs.) The beautiful groupie Miss Pamela, erstwhile queen of the legendary GTOs, was in a corner talking to someone I thought might be Keith Moon. The hippie cocaine merchant was on duty and in his glory—dealer to Led Zeppelin!—although I was told that Robert had declined to purchase the old Chevy. The band disappeared into the bathroom for their lines, and I went into the hall to try to find a seat.

For me, and probably for the band, the show was a letdown, and fell apart after the high energy of the first three songs, sonic tracers competing with the din of the strings of lit firecrackers that kids were throwing at the stage that sounded like gunshots when they were broadcast by the stage microphones. Plant was coked up and garrulous from the stage, chanting "a gram is a gram is a gram," probably not in homage to the late Gertrude Stein. He told the crowd that these shows, the final ones on the first leg of the American tour, were important to them. He said he was glad the tour wasn't ending in New York like in 1973, when Led Zeppelin's hotel safe was robbed of $180,000 in cash. He remarked that John Bonham had decided not to have a sex change operation after all. He insulted Bad Company singer Paul Rogers.

Robert had begun to interpolate sections of "Gallows Pole" into "Trampled Under Foot" in Seattle, and he continued this in

L.A. The band took a long "breather" during another half hour of "Moby Dick." I tried to get backstage myself to grab a beer but was stopped at the curtain for having a yellow pass. After "Moby Dick," a newly refreshed, Peruvian-inspired Robert took the microphone: "What a *wonderful* drum solo! And what a *wonderful* blow job in the dressing room. Thank you—*Ahmet Ertegun!*"

The doom wallow of "Dazed and Confused" was next, all oozing vocals and stygian murk produced with the violin bow. But the band seemed tired, and Robert wasn't hitting those high notes of old. The encores almost made up for it. The Zeppelin dynamited the hall with both "Black Dog" and "Heartbreaker," sending their audience into the humid night with the sound of proto-grunge ringing in their ears.

Two nights off. In the Riot House bar on Wednesday night, the waitress (short skirt, net stockings, aspiring actress from Memphis, very glam and cute) told me she'd heard that the Led Zeppelin drummer had gone on a rampage, smashed up his suite, passed out drunk with a lit cigarette, catching the bed on fire. Sprinklers went off. The fire trucks came at four in the morning. Another rumor had it that the tour doctor had left after accusing Jimmy, or someone, of taking drugs from his medical bags.

The obsolete backstage pass got me into the back door of the Forum again on Thursday, March 25. There was less glamour and celebrity backstage, which is probably why Led Zeppelin played so much better that night. Robert seemed to confirm the Bonzo rumor when he introduced him as the man who broke every pane of glass in room 1019 . . . "the man who set fire to his own bed . . . that amazing man . . . Mr. Quaalude!" He dedicated

"Stairway to Heaven" to all of the band's English friends who were staying at the Riot House, on Led Zeppelin's tab. "Kashmir" was about "places where the red light still shines for two rupees, places where there's magic in the air."

"Dazed and Confused" lasted forty minutes. I know because I kept looking at my watch. In the middle, Page played some flamenco riffs, which morphed into a few bars of "Spanish Harlem." The theremin show was thrilling, with Page gesturing through sustained electronic thunder like he was wielding the transmitter of the gods.

After "Black Dog," the L E D Z E P P E L I N sign flashed on as the band took their bows amid human thunder from the customers. Robert: "Thank you, people of the Forum. We've had a good time tonight." And they were gone.

The yellow pass failed me on the final night of the tour: Saturday, March 27, 1975. A different stage door guard was even comparing IDs with a guest list, so I didn't bother trying. The box office had nothing, so I got a rafter seat—miles from the stage—for $25 from a scalper. It was a new, wide-angle perspective on a scene I'd witnessed from as close as possible.

The evening's concert, which went on an hour late, was introduced by Linda Lovelace, the actress most famous for performing fellatio in the movie *Deep Throat*. Crazy, dangerous firecrackers were again thrown at the band, who stayed mostly out of range. To compensate the fans, and it being the end of the tour, Led Zeppelin played for three and a half hours. "Since I've Been Loving You" was again inserted between "Kashmir" and "No Quarter." ("Kashmir," Robert advised, was about "the waste lands . . . the wasted lands . . . and I don't mean the lobby of the Continental Riot House either.") For the encores, scurrying roadies set up another drum kit and Badco's Simon Kirke sat in with John Bonham for "Whole Lotta Love" with an astonishing musique concrète "middle section" by Jimmy Page that seemed to sum up all the hard work, homesickness, freezing weather, night flights, laser lights, sprains and illnesses, orgasms and addictions, power trips and rampages, lonely nights and unsatisfying, often distraught phone calls to a faraway home on the other side of the world over a bad connection that went into putting on a rock & roll tour.

When the cheering subsided, and it was announced that the band had left the building, I sat for a while at the top of the great arena as it slowly emptied. I could hardly believe that the PA was playing songs from *The Harder They Come*. The empty floor revealed hundreds of discarded shoes, clothing, and underwear.

There was a party at the Riot House to mark the tour's end. I didn't attend, but my cocktail waitress friend did, as the date of a Badco member whose name she didn't know, and she told me the champagne was the best she'd ever had, and she got everyone's autograph.

CHAPTER 36

Hardest Core Rock

A few days later, I flew home to write about my journey with Led Zeppelin. First I caught up with the press accounts concerning the tour I'd missed. Cameron Crowe's *Rolling Stone* article duly valorized Led Zeppelin as avatars of hard-rock sainthood. As expected, the young reporter had crowbarred some star-quality quotations out of Robert Plant and Jimmy Page. (I was impressed.) In *Rolling Stone*'s next issue, critic Jim Miller reversed the magazine's longtime distaste for the English band in a long meditation titled "Anglo Graffiti: Hardest Core Rock." Calling Led Zeppelin "the world's most popular band," and *Physical Graffiti* a tour de force, Miller for the first time demanded that Jimmy Page be recognized as a masterful, even brilliant record producer. Page, he wrote, "could probably arrange a quartet of finger cymbals and have it come lumbering out of the loudspeakers sounding like Led Zeppelin. . . . They have forged an original style, and have now grown within it; they have rooted their music in hard-core rock & roll, and yet have gone beyond it. They may not be the greatest rock band of the seventies, but they must be counted among them."

Over the next two weeks, I transcribed my interviews and typed up my notes. I submitted my article, titled "At the Riot House with Led Zeppelin," to my editor at *The Atlantic Monthly*. Two weeks later, he informed me that the magazine's elderly editor in chief absolutely hated my piece. He was particularly offended at my mention of the mirror ball, which the band had hung over the audience in their arena shows, noting that mirror balls had been common among the swing bands of his distant youth. Also, the old fart had apparently listened to a Led Zeppelin album, or as much as he could stand, and had told my editor it wasn't music but the death agonies of screaming monkeys.

I didn't care. *The Atlantic Monthly* assignment was just an excuse to get a seat on the Starship, the benefits of which would obviously be revealed at some future date. I called Danny Goldberg, but he didn't care about it either. The magazine paid me a kill fee for not publishing the piece. I secured my bulging Zeppelin file, put it in a drawer for safekeeping, and used the kill fee to buy a plane ticket to Jamaica, where Bob Marley and his fellow reggae stars were most hospitable when Peter Simon and I went down there to report on them for *The New York Times* a few months later.

Led Zeppelin stayed in Los Angeles instead of going home. The band's exile was explained to the curious rock press as necessary, because Britain's Inland Revenue taxed the big rock stars' song-publishing royalty income at an appalling 95 percent in some cases. This was untenable for the biggest bands because the record industry was corrupt, and publishing rights were the only sure way of insuring income from their recordings, other than going on the road and playing for people as musicians had always done.

Meanwhile, Grant began to schedule Led Zeppelin's second American tour of 1975, to begin in August at the Rose Bowl, the big football stadium in Pasadena. A lot of these shows were in secondary markets, where the band had missed first time around or had never played before. Bill Graham got two big shows at the Oakland Coliseum Stadium, with the Pretty Things opening, and Joe Walsh as a special guest. When tickets went on sale for these shows a few weeks later, they sold out in a few minutes.

For the next month, Led Zeppelin settled into the L.A music scene. They went to industry parties. At one, Jimmy Page chatted with Joni Mitchell, one of Zeppelin's heroes. At another party, Peter Grant introduced himself to Bob Dylan as Zeppelin's manager. "I don't tell you my problems," Dylan drawled. "Don't tell me yours."

In April, Swan Song threw a big party at the Shrine Auditorium to introduce the Pretty Things to the L.A. media. Robert had appeared with the Pretties in a taped TV segment that was later broadcast on the syndicated *Midnight Special* program. The party went well until a drunken Bonzo assaulted and screamed at a London journalist who had wanted to tell the drummer how much he admired his work. A crazed Bonzo had to be pulled away from the poor man.

John Bonham wasn't cut out to be a tax exile, like Elton and Mick. He missed his family, was lonely and depressed. He had a local girlfriend who tried to look after him, but she was pretty useless at keeping the demon down. He dealt with this by stay-

ing drunk all the time, which led to psychotic outbursts and violent episodes. Over the remainder of 1975, he was involved in
several ugly scenes in Los Angeles. In one, he attacked a well-
known woman on the local music scene who had smiled at him
in a bar, hitting her and knocking her off her chair. He attacked
a clerk at Tower Records and was almost arrested, but the store
manager said they wouldn't press charges. He got into it outside
the Rainbow with the doorman, a short man who didn't look to
be any trouble. Bonzo was a big guy and usually bullied people
only when he had roadies or minders around to back him up.
This time he was alone, and the little doorman turned out to be
a karate black belt. John swung at him, and he was hit so hard in
return that he went down like the sack of shit he was when he
was drunk. Bonzo's eyes were so black after this fight that Peter
Grant insisted he be taken to Cedars-Sinai Medical Center to
make sure he wouldn't die later from a blood clot in his brain.
Led Zeppelin wasn't invited to any more exclusive Hollywood
parties after that. The Beast's behavior in those days dragged
Led Zeppelin's reputation to hell and beyond.

A month later, Led Zeppelin went home to play five nights at
Earls Court Exhibition Centre, then the biggest room in England.
The original three shows sold out in moments, so two more were
added. Led Zeppelin would bring its "American Show"—lights,
fog, and lasers—to the UK for the first time during five nights in
May 1975. The production was too expensive to lug around the
country on a normal rock tour, so Led Zeppelin would play for
85,000 fans in one spot, make a pile of money, and then skip
back to California before Inland Revenue dunned them for over-
staying their statutory limits.

Texas-based production company Showco air-freighted Led Zeppelin's entire American stage set to London, at crucifying expense. The serious change in electric current proved daunting when it was tested on a soundstage at Shepperton Studios for many days, and in the end the laser lights would be only half as bright as in North America. But Led Zeppelin felt they were so hot, after two months of playing, that the group's very honor demanded the British audience be exposed to their current incarnation. Earl's Court was a cavernous exhibition hall, so the promoter installed two 24-by-30-foot video screens on either side of the stage so the people in back could see what was going on. Nothing like this had been done in England before, adding another level of hoopla.

Led Zeppelin was back in England by May 10, at home after five months. The band actually rehearsed for the London shows; an acoustic set had been added in the middle of the show. This interlude would begin (improbably) with Led Zeppelin singing a four-part harmony on never-before-performed *LZ III* track "Tangerine" for five nights in London. According to Robert Plant, whose idea this was, the band worked very hard on getting it right. A doctor showed up at one of the rehearsals to inoculate Jimmy and Robert against cholera, typhus, and hepatitis because they were going to Morocco after the London shows to do some research for *Led Zeppelin VII.*

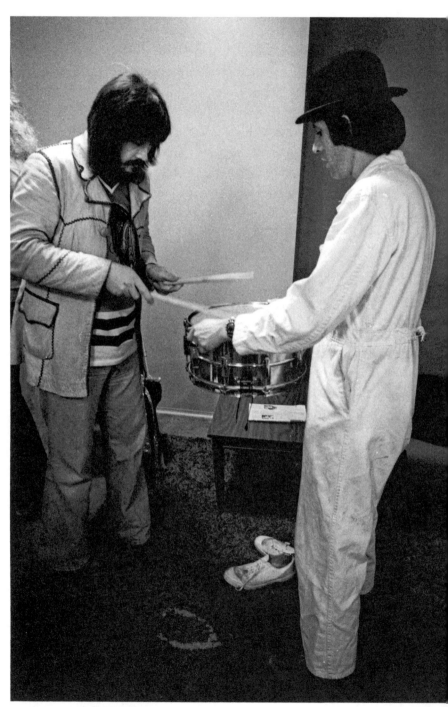

BONHAM WITH LZ ROADIE MICK HINTON

CHAPTER 37

The Exiles Return

The first show was Saturday, May 17, and was typical of the rest. "Rock and Roll" began the battle, melding into "Sick Again" from *Physical Graffiti*. After "Over the Hills," Robert would do stand-up comedy while Led Zeppelin shed its booster rockets and Jimmy took up his old, cheap Sears Roebuck Danelectro guitar. Most nights, Robert dedicated "In My Time of Dying" to the Labour Party's treasury minister, Denis Healey, who was charged with carrying out the draconian tax laws that drove England's wealthiest citizens away from home and discouraged rock stars and other entrepreneurs from doing their best work in their own country. These were the definitive performances of the episodic "Dying," with Jimmy gesturing through the sustained chords of the flu-fever drones, and then channeling the late James Marshall Hendrix for a quarter hour of murderous guitar dynamism.

Jimmy deployed his two-necked red Gibson guitar for "The

Song Remains the Same" and "The Rain Song." After hyperdra-
matized "Kashmir" and cod-jazzy "No Quarter," it was time for
the new, mid-concert acoustic set. This saw three-fourths of Led
Zeppelin sitting in chairs under spotlights. Jimmy had a Martin
D-28 guitar, Jones a mandolin, Plant a harmonica. "Tangerine"
came off fey, disorganized, a little strange, finally endearing—Led
Zepp eats Fairport Convention. Jimmy played rhythm guitar, and
Jones expertly finger-picked the Joni Mitchell homage "Going to
California." John Paul's mandolin also dominated a pretty "That's
the Way" (from *LZ III*). But Jimmy Page woke up and played ex-
tended, scrolling bluegrass guitar licks on rollicking "Bron-Y-Aur
Stomp," with John Paul Jones playing an unusual upright electro-
acoustic bass. "Stomp" was the only Led Zeppelin song on which
John Bonham ever had a vocal role, and the tapes show he sang
credibly with his best friend, Robert Plant, during all five nights
in London.

After the acoustic set, the band stretched out the shows.
"Trampled Under Foot" got Page's hardest-jamming solos of the
tour, looping skeins of brilliant, show-off guitar. "No Quarter"
and "Dazed" went on for eons. "Stairway" was now offered like
a solemn requiem for another era—a faithful recitation of a classic anthem—which in a way it was.

The five nights had, of course, variants in comedy routines
and improvisations. First night (Saturday, May 17), the regular
set was concentrated and red hot, but the acoustic songs were
ragged, unsure. Jimmy salvaged the concert with exuberant, even
excessive (and this would be noticed) variations, and then taught
a heavy-metal guitar clinic during an over-the-top "Whole Lotta
Love."

Sunday, May 18: Robert Plant, after the third song: "Good
evening. We are more than overjoyed . . . to be allowed back into

the country." This tax exile's ironic greeting met with tepid response from an audience hard-pressed by the recessionary economic climate of 1975 England, where almost everyone was struggling in the wake of an Arab oil embargo and predatory labor strikes that left England threadbare and occasionally unheated that winter. But clueless Robert, who'd been living in America, followed this with more bitter commentary about politicians and taxation, insipid stage patter perhaps unique in the history of the twentieth-century rock movement. He also mentioned that his arm hurt because of the inoculations. Robert announced that he and Jimmy were "going hunting in the jungle for new words and new songs for a new album." Robert also had a problem in the acoustic set. The previous evening, he'd sung "Bron-Y-Aur Stomp" while holding a handwritten lyric sheet. But the crib was missing on this show, Robert complained, and he'd only gotten through the song by following Bonzo, who knew the lyric by heart.

The third night, Friday, May 23, was the perfect Led Zeppelin show. Everything clicked, including the acoustic set. Robert name-checked inspirational British troubadour Roy Harper, who was attending Earl's Court every night, and publicly asked him to start paying for his tickets. More to the point, John Bonham ran the show like a general, playing brutal rhythms that nevertheless had the girls in the sold-out audience swinging their hips, if not baring their breasts like their distant cousins in San Diego. Plant introduced the drummer as ". . . my worst friend, the one who kicks me when I'm down."

The fourth night, Jimmy Page turned "Trampled Under Foot" into a maelstrom of rock guitar mannerisms, supported by John Bonham's mastodon energy. The surviving videos and bootleg recordings of this show illustrate that the perfectly matched duality—Page and Bonham—orbited the moon that night, returned to earth, and lived to tell the tale. The inescapable conclusion among some hard-core fans is that Led Zeppelin never got any better than this.

But the band thought the last night was the best. The tapes reveal that they played with an easy familiarity with the set they'd deployed since the freezing nights of January in Chicago, when all of them had felt ill. Now the performance was almost second nature, and Jimmy Page feinted and reared like a cobra ready to strike. "Dazed and Confused" was given a performance so volcanic and excessive that it may have contributed to the hard fact that it was never performed in public again by Led Zeppelin. "Stairway to Heaven" was almost crushed by multiple lashings of Hendrix quotes, thunderous cascades of tumbling notes, and intricate arabesques of blues guitar. To end the Earl's Court residency, Led Zeppelin segued "Black Dog" into "Communication Breakdown," bringing their audience to heart-attack level before sending them home with more ill-advised ranting from Robert Plant about their tax situation. He thanked the customers for "five glorious days" at Earl's Court. "Thanks for being a great audience. And if you see Denis Healey . . . *Tell him that we're gone.*"

Reaction to Led Zeppelin's star turn in London was mixed at best. Friends in the press lauded their visionary ideas and battle-hardened musical chops. Tony Palmer rhapsodized in the influential *Observer*: "By remaining calm at the center of a disintegrating culture, [Page] is providing an example for its future development. If we need heroes, then rather Jimmy Page than political buffoons or sporting apes; rather the shy, nervous, steely youth whose songs are inspiring a generation."

But others were horrified by the idea that Led Zeppelin's unstable virtuosity might point to the future, especially in music. The next generation of punk-loving kids was appalled by the bloated, expensive display at Earl's Court, where the fans were as far removed from the musicians as crowds at a football match. In England at least, the future would demand new bands who actually were their own audience. Now Zeppelin and the spangled old rock bands provoked a lurid, viral movement where you didn't even have to play three chords on your guitar to become on overnight hero of a new subculture that reviled Led Zeppelin as one of the obsolete breed—Boring Old Farts.

Led Zeppelin fled this England after these shows, and set up in Montreux, Switzerland, where they were looked after by a local music promoter. Robert Plant and Jimmy Page then met up in Morocco and drove through the mighty Atlas Mountains and then around the former Spanish Sahara for a while, seeking inspiration for the album they were due to write and record later in the year.

Back in Montreux, they had a meeting to discuss plans. The summer/fall American tour was now up to thirty concerts. Promoters in South America were offering big money to play there for the first time. Japan also offered unlimited yen for another visit by the Zeppelin, and Australia was calling too. Robert wanted to return to Morocco and record Berber music. Jimmy spoke of doing the same in Cairo and India. Led Zeppelin's wealth and freedom of movement offered them the planet on a plate. Finally, everything was going their way.

And then, of course, it happened. It almost had to.

Chapter 38

The Hard Road to Presence

Like a mythic tale of hubris among the ancient gods, Led Zeppelin met its destiny on the Greek island of Rhodes, as it baked in the wine-dark Aegean Sea in the summer of 1975. Jimmy Page and Robert Plant had taken their women and children to the island for a summer holiday on the advice of Phil May of the Pretty Things, who had a house there. On August 3, Jimmy left briefly to visit an old property for sale in Sicily with strong associations to Aleister Crowley. The next day, August 4, Maureen Plant was driving home from the beach. Robert was in the front seat. Their two children and Jimmy's daughter were in back. The car swerved, left the road, careered down an embankment, and smashed into a tree. Everyone was screaming except for Maureen. Robert thought she looked dead. His leg was shattered and he couldn't get out of the car. The kids were bruised, banged up, and crying.

At the hospital, when they finally got there, the doctors told Robert that his leg was broken, and his wife was in grave condition because her skull had fractured. Jimmy's girlfriend Charlotte Martin began a series of frantic phone calls. Peter Grant was also on holiday and couldn't be reached. She finally got through to Richard Cole, told him that Robert, Maureen, and the children were dying, and that he had to get them out of there immediately.

It took Cole a while, but he managed to organize a private jet and flew to Rhodes with two doctors and a supply of Maureen's rare blood type. The medical situation was dire, and the police wanted to know if Maureen had been drunk or on drugs. With a couple of rented cars, the piratical Cole swooped down on the hospital, paid the bill in cash, and spirited the English patients to the airport, where their jet took off for London.

The doctors managed to stabilize Maureen, and the Black Country Woman survived. Robert's ankle was broken, along with one of his elbows. He was told it would be six months before he could walk unaided. (Hey hey, Mama, what's the matter here?)

Peter Grant returned to England and canceled the rest of the 1975 American tour. Meanwhile, Robert had to be gotten out of the country or his nonresident tax status would be erased and he'd lose a fortune. So at the last moment, Robert and his wheelchair were flown to Jersey, the English Channel island whose laws exempted him from persecution by Her Majesty's taxman.

Led Zeppelin convened on Jersey and decided what to do. The band would return to California, where they would write the next Zeppelin album. The concert film they had begun during the 1973 tour would be revived and given a theatrical release to try to compensate for the loss of tour income for what looked to be two years. They were all amazed at this abrupt reversal of fortune, but they had no choice other than to curse the gods and accept their fate.

In September 1975, Led Zeppelin returned to California. After a few days in the Riot House, they decamped to rented beach houses on Malibu Colony Drive. Robert was reportedly freaked out that his band's accrued negativity—singing "In My Time of Dying" every night—had affected his family. Jimmy Page was using heroin, and nodded off at a photo call for the band Detective, a new Swan Song signing. John Bonham was lurching his drunken way around the Sunset Strip like Frankenstein's monster. John Paul Jones was off by himself, avoiding everyone in the now obviously doomed Zeppelin camp, showing up only for the album run-throughs when they began that October at SIR studios in West Hollywood.

And these ran very hot. The energy that would have been expended on the second leg of the American tour went into the new music instead. Poetic cadences that echoed the chanting of *The Iliad* were matched with bolero variations and the New Orleans "second line" rhythm. Guilt-laden blues laments were paired with clarion riffs heard on the streets of Marrakesh. John Bonham may have been crazy when drunk, but he always appeared sober at the rehearsals, and was playing at a high level, with an intense rubbery funk. Robert told a reporter that his lyrics reflected a new man, one burnt by the sun for coming too close, and lucky to come away from it only singed, with his family intact and alive.

But then Led Zeppelin had to leave America or pay tax to the Internal Revenue Service. In November, the gypsy band reconvened in Munich, Germany, in a studio owned by Euro-disco magnate Giorgio Moroder. Jimmy had two weeks to make an album before the Rolling Stones were scheduled at the studio to make their first record with new guitarist Ron Wood.

Led Zeppelin tore into it with demonic fervor. Jimmy's obsessive perfectionism was forced to be tight but loose. Robert was out of his wheelchair and hobbling with a cane. This would be an up-tempo, epic voyage of an album, taking its listeners on a journey that risked the safety of the sheltering sky for the terrors of the vast, uncharted Beyond.

"Achilles Last Stand" was the best achievement of Jimmy Page's longtime ambition to build a cathedral of chiming guitars over a narrative of some kind of epic grandeur. "For Your Life" was about the cocaine-fueled demimonde of the Hollywood rock world, and captured its glamorous desperation with vibrational accuracy. "Royal Orleans" was an inside joke about John Paul Jones, set to an accelerated rumba by John Bonham that shook like a levee-breaking earthquake.

Led Zeppelin's take on Blind Willie Johnson's "Nobody's Fault but Mine" captured the band's essential genius in its darkest hour to date. The monkey on the back, the deal with the devil, the heroin and cocaine, the exile and disillusion were all nobody else's fault. Led Zeppelin finally owned itself, warts and all, in this blistering new music. Other tracks were no less cool. "Candy Store Rock" was L.A. psychobilly, a unique rock hybrid never heard before, or since. "Hots On for Nowhere" had a blitzkrieg riff that would define glam/hair metal in years to come. And the long, bluesy dirge, "Tea for One," was an unsparing self-portrait of rock stars at the end of their emotional rope, rich but emotionally desolate young men operating under intense pressure, without the anchor of their families, and a long, long way from home.

The Stones were coming in, but the record wasn't done.

Mick Jagger gave Jimmy a couple of extra days, and Page played the entire album's fractious, exhilarating guitar solos in twenty-four hours. The album would be called *Presence* and would be released a few months later, in 1976.

Led Zeppelin never made a better record.

December was the end of tumultuous, life-changing 1975 for Led Zeppelin and its people. After Munich, still in exile, they huddled in Jersey until they could go home for the Christmas holidays. Jimmy Page flew to New York to work on the now crucial Led Zeppelin movie. On New Year's Eve, Robert Plant walked across his kitchen, without a stick, for the first time since the summer car wreck. The next years would bring new challenges, which would somehow be met. Led Zeppelin would survive for almost five more years until their luck ran out and the devil finally called in the loan.

Friends of LZ

CHAPTER 39

Clean and Purifying Riffs

I pretty much forgot about Led Zeppelin for a while. Then, in the spring of 1976, I heard that the new Rolling Stones album, *Black and Blue*, was about to come out. This was the record the Stones made in Munich after Led Zeppelin cleared out. I called *Rolling Stone*'s music editor, Dave Marsh, and asked if I could review the Stones for the magazine. I hadn't written for Dave since the previous October, when I had reviewed Mirabai's album. Danny and Swan Song had sent Mirabai to record in Nashville with an important producer, arranger, and top session musicians. But she was unable to translate her reverent pan-spirituality into songs that fit any of the commercial formats of the day. No one in Led Zeppelin wanted to release her music on Swan Song, so Mirabai's album came out on Atlantic Records instead. Of course I gave her a good notice, mostly in tribute to all the faith and hard work Danny Goldberg had put into her project.

Now Dave Marsh told me that he was going to review *Black and Blue*, and he was going to say it was not the Rolling Stones' best work. I could review the new Led Zeppelin record instead if I wanted to. Soon an advance pressing of *Presence* was mailed to me, and once again I brewed some tea, had a pipe, put on the headphones, and dropped the needle into the groove.

When I took the headphones off, after side two, my ears were smoking.

My review of *Presence* ran in the May 20, 1976, issue of *Rolling Stone* as follows:

Led Zeppelin's seventh album confirms this quartet's status as heavy-metal champions of the known universe. Presence *takes up where last season's monumentally molten* Physical Graffiti *left off—few melodies, a preoccupation with hard-rock rhythm, lengthy echoing moans gushing from Robert Plant and a lyrical slant toward the cosmos. (Give an Englishman 50,000 watts, a chartered jet, plenty of cocaine and some groupies and he thinks he's a god. It's getting to be an old story.)*

Physical Graffiti *was an ultimate record of sorts ("Trampled Under Foot" was the hardest rock ever played by humans, while "Kashmir" must be the most pompous) and the new record certainly tries to keep up. The opening track, "Achilles Last Stand," could be the Yardbirds ten years down the road. The format is familiar: John Bonham's furiously attacking drums is really the lead instrument, until Jimmy Page tires of chording under Robert Plant and takes over.*

Although Page and Plant are masters of the form, emotions sometimes conflict and the results are mixed. A few bars from one piece convince the listener that he's hearing the greatest rock & roll ever, then the very next few place him in a nightmarish 1970 movie about deranged hippies.

Actually there is some fine rock on Presence. *"Nobody's Fault but Mine" is strong, while "Candy Store Rock" perfectly evokes the Los Angeles milieu in which Led Zeppelin composed this album; it sounds like an unholy hybrid in which the head of Buddy Holly is grafted onto the quivering stem of David Bowie.*

Zeppelin's main concern is to establish a reliable riff and stick to it, without complicating things too much with melody or nuance. At their best, the riffs are clean and purifying. The two dreary examples of blooze ("Tea for One," "For Your Life") may stretch even the diehard fan's loyalty, but make no mistake: Presence *is another monster in what by now is a continuing tradition of battles won by this band of survivors.*

For the record, more than thirty years later, *Presence* is still my favorite Led Zeppelin album.

Zeppilogue

Many fans of classic rock, those weaned on its legends and lore, will be sad to learn that you can no longer throw a television off the balcony of the Riot House and watch it shatter into shards of glass and plastic in the street below.

I visited the newly renovated hotel, now called the Andaz West Hollywood, after it reopened in 2009. The entire façade of the building, facing Sunset Boulevard, had been encased behind a trendy glass curtain wall. The famous balconies became enclosed sunrooms whose windows don't open wide enough to defenestrate even a flat-screen TV, should you manage to pry it off the wall in a Beast-like fury.

Over time, Led Zeppelin also was encased under glass, encased in legends and lore; absolute monarchs of classic rock radio; floating in a timeless fame continuum as the best, the heaviest, rock band ever. Led Zeppelin set an unattainable standard of both virtuosity and excess for those adepts and seekers who tried to follow their path. Of course, we know that no other band ever got even close, leaving Zeppelin alone in the virtual arena as still-reigning world champions of rock.

Some say that, like many great champions, Led Zeppelin retired undefeated.

I don't think Robert Plant feels that way.

As we've seen in the prologue to this story, there were some tempting offers for Led Zeppelin to regroup, after a successful 2007 benefit concert in London proved that the three aging rock stars (and the son of their late drummer) could still perform their old songs and sound like Led Zeppelin. The financial rewards were going to be unprecedented; the fame incalculable; the music exalted beyond its already magisterial and widely acknowledged position as the greatest body of work any rock band ever produced.

Robert Plant walked away from this, and for good reason. He obviously gave it some thought. Reviving Led Zeppelin would have put on hold a successful, award-winning Americana/Bluegrass band he was enjoying with a beautiful Illinois belle, Alison Krauss. Plant was already on record that he couldn't see himself stumbling around football stadiums with Led Zeppelin anymore.

The very idea of a Led Zeppelin tour must have brought back terrible and heartbreaking memories for him. During the last one, in 1980, John Bonham drank himself to death. Plant, Page, and Jones decided they couldn't go on, and that was the end of the band.

Before that was the nightmarish Led Zeppelin tour of 1977, aborted after drug addiction, diabolic violence, and the mysterious death of Robert's young son, at home in England, made it impossible to continue.

Peter Grant had died in 1995. What would Led Zeppelin

look like in the twenty-first century except a "band of survivors" tempting the fates one more time.

Some Led Zeppelin fans had to be relieved when Robert Plant walked away.

Most fans have a favorite Led Zeppelin. For the older ones who saw them first, it's the unstoppable, near-savage head bangers of 1969. For others, it's the pillaging marauders of 1970. Some prefer the folkish, esoteric bluesmen who created the electric madrigals of 1971. The most rabid fans love the Zeppelin of 1972, the year the West was won. Tens of thousands were blown away by the generational nostalgia and emotional power of the famous Knebworth Festival concerts in 1979.

My favorite Led Zeppelin will always be LZ-'75. It was a rough-and-tumble year. You had to be there.

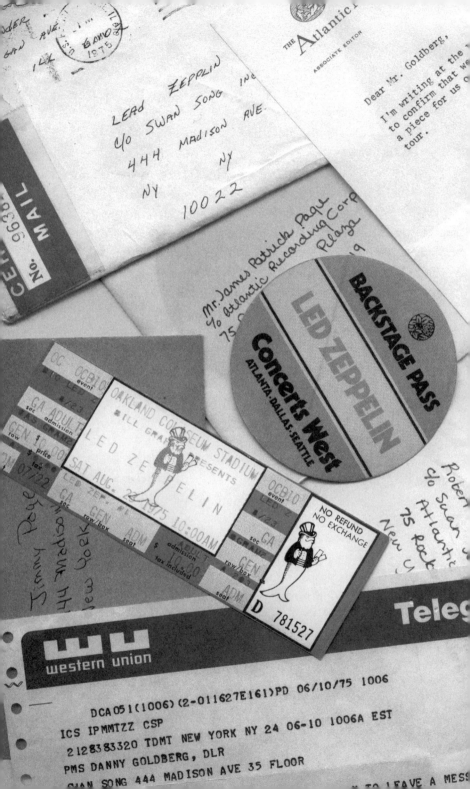

Acknowledgments

Thanks to everyone who helped, especially in 1975: Peter Simon, Danny Goldberg, David Silver, David Doubilet, Anne L. Doubilet, Stu Werbin, Bob Palmer, and William Burroughs.

Thanks to everyone at Gotham Books, especially publisher Bill Shinker, editor Lauren Marino, and inspired Texas Ranger Travers Johnson, who saw this project through to press.

Mike Harriot: Traveler of Time and Space.

And my inspiring and indispensable muses, including Chris Davis, JHA, Hana and Howard, Lily Aisha, India Lucy, Penelope LaCalicot, James Isaacs, Ande Zellman, David Bieber, #12-C at 501, Casey Ferrell-Tillotson, Mr. and Mrs. Nelson, and David and Maria at Leonard Stephen Inc.

Naturam expellas furca, tamen usque recurret.